THE FREEDOM RIDES AND ALABAMA

ROUTE OF 1947 JOURNEY OF RECONCILIATION

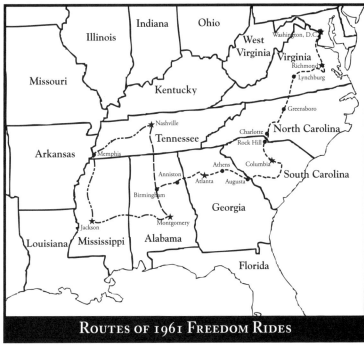

ROUTES OF 1961 FREEDOM RIDES

THE
FREEDOM RIDES
AND
ALABAMA

**A Guide to Key
Events and Places,
Context, and Impact**

NOELLE MATTESON

PUBLISHED BY
NewSouth Books
MONTGOMERY | LOUISVILLE

IN COLLABORATION WITH
The Alabama Historical Commission

NewSouth Books
105 S. Court Street
Montgomery, AL 36104

Library of Congress Cataloging-in-Publication Data

Matteson, Noelle.
The Freedom Rides and Alabama : a guide to key events and places,
context, and impact / Noelle Matteson.

p. cm.

Includes bibliographical references and index.

ISBN-13: 978-1-60306-106-3
ISBN-10: 1-60306-106-1

1. Freedom Rides, 1961. 2. African Americans—Civil rights—
Alabama—History—20th century. 3. Civil rights movements—
Alabama—History—20th century. 4. Historic sites—Alabama.
5. Museums—Alabama. 6. Memorials—Alabama. 7. Alabama—
History, Local. 8. Alabama—Race relations—History—20th century.
I. Alabama Historical Commission. II. Title.
E185.93.A3M28 2011
323.1196'0730761—dc23

2011022226

Second Printing

Printed in the United States of America

For more information on Freedom Rides events,
visit www.newsouthbooks.com.

Timeline

1947 — Journey of Reconciliation

April 9	Virginia: Riders leave Washington, D.C., for Richmond.
April 10	Arrival at Petersburg. Conrad Lynn arrested.
April 11	North Carolina: Trailways bus arrives at Raleigh. Greyhound bus arrives at Durham.
April 12	Bayard Rustin, James Peck, and Andrew Johnson arrested in Durham. Arrival at Chapel Hill.
April 13	Rustin, Johnson, Peck, Joseph Felmet, and Igal Roodenko arrested in Chapel Hill.
April 13	Trailways bus arrives in Greensboro.
April 14	Greyhound bus arrives in Winston-Salem.
April 15	Buses pass through Statesville. Trailways bus arrives in Asheville.
April 16	Peck and Dennis Banks arrested in Asheville.
April 17	Tennessee: Trailways bus arrives in Knoxville. Greyhound bus arrives in Nashville.
April 18	Kentucky: Greyhound bus arrives in Louisville.
April 19	One Greyhound bus leaves from Weaversville, N.C. Train Riders make overnight stops in West Virginia and Kentucky.
April 20	Virginia: Greyhound and train Riders arrive in Roanoke.
April 21	Greyhound and train Riders arrive in Lynchburg.
April 22	Several arrested in Amherst and Culpeper.
April 23	Arrival in Washington, D.C.

1961 — CORE Freedom Ride

May 4	Virginia: Riders leave Washington, D.C., for Richmond.

May 5	Arrival in Petersburg.
May 6	Riders pass through Farmville and Lynchburg.
May 7	North Carolina: Arrival in Danville and Greensboro.
May 8	Riders pass through High Point, Salisbury, and Charlotte, where Joseph Perkins is arrested.
May 9	South Carolina: Arrival in Rock Hill, where John Lewis is attacked.
May 10	Arrivals in Winnsboro, where Hank Thomas and Peck are arrested, and Columbia.
May 10-11	Arrivals in Sumter.
May 12	Georgia: Arrival in Augusta.
May 13	Riders pass through Athens and meet Martin Luther King, Jr. in Atlanta.
May 14	Alabama: Riders attacked in Anniston and Birmingham.
May 15	Louisiana: Original riders fly to New Orleans.
May 16-17	Riders in New Orleans.

Reinforcements

May 17	Alabama: Riders leave from Nashville for Birmingham, where they are arrested.
May 18	Bull Connor takes riders to state line.
May 19	Riders driven from Ardmore back to Birmingham.
May 20	Riders arrive in Montgomery, where they are attacked.
May 21-22	Mass meeting in First Baptist Church.
May 24	Mississippi: Riders leave Montgomery for Jackson, where they are arrested.
June 15	Riders transferred to Parchman Prison Farm.
July 7	First group of riders leave Parchman.
Nov 1	ICC announces desegregation of interstate bus facilities.

CONTENTS

FOREWORD

By ARLAM CARR JR.

I was too young to be a Freedom Rider, but I well remember when they arrived in Montgomery. My parents, Johnnie and Arlam Carr Sr., had been active in the Montgomery black community long before the Montgomery Bus Boycott. Mama, in fact, was a childhood friend of Rosa Parks, and it was at Mama's urging that Mrs. Parks became active with the NAACP in the 1940s.

So when the Freedom Rides began, there was excitement and anticipation in our house. We all knew how important the riders' challenge to segregation really was. After the rioting by the white mob at the Greyhound bus station on Saturday, May 21, 1961, Mama insisted on going to the First Baptist Church on Ripley Street for the mass meeting called in response.

When white rabble-rousers began rioting outside the church, too, Mama was among the people who were trapped and had to spend the night inside the church while federal marshals and the National Guard tried to restore order outside. Meanwhile, Dr. Martin Luther King was in the church basement on the phone to U.S. Attorney General Robert Kennedy asking for protection.

These events, as we now know, played a pivotal role in breaking down Jim Crow segregation and also helped push Kennedy and his brother, President John F. Kennedy, toward a more vigorous position with respect to civil rights. Locally, the principled courage of the freedom riders, contrasted with the lawless response of the white mobs, helped change the political climate in Montgomery and some white moderate voices emerged on the side of peaceful desegregation.

Mama eventually became president of the Montgomery Improvement Association — Dr. King was its first president — and in the 1980s she and the MIA helped in the crusade to keep the Greyhound bus station from being torn down at the time the annex to the federal courthouse was being built on the adjacent property. Mama and the MIA, Judge Myron Thompson, the Alabama Historical Commission, and Congressman John Lewis were among those who believed that because of what had happened there, the Greyhound bus station should be preserved as a reminder of the historical significance of the Freedom Rides.

Mama did not live to see the new Freedom Rides Museum that has now opened in the old bus station, but she would have been proud to see what has been accomplished in its first phase and what may be added as the future plans come to fruition

She knew that what the freedom riders did in 1961 was brave and necessary, and she welcomed the changes that came to interstate transportation as a result.

I am delighted to help introduce this brief guidebook to the events, places, and people of the Freedom Rides. This book gives only a summary history of the Freedom Rides, but it focuses on the events that took place in Alabama.

I believe it is important that we remember not only what happened in Montgomery, but why the Riders came here, and what

---

Arlam Carr Jr. was the named plaintiff in the 1964 lawsuit that desegregated the public schools in Montgomery, Alabama, and became one of the first black graduates of Sidney Lanier High School. He attended the University of Texas at El Paso and has worked in television news production for going on four decades.

*Rosa Parks, right, and her friend Johnnie Carr, on a ceremonial
anniversary ride on a Montgomery city bus, 1975.*

happened as a result of their coming. The story of the Freedom
Rides is well known now in a general sense, but the details of Jim
Crow laws, the particular moment when the Freedom Riders decided to challenge them, and the amazing story of the events that
ensued — all of this history is not well understood by the public
and deserves to be. That is why this guide, and the museum in
Montgomery that it accompanies, is such a useful introduction.

PREFACE

This book was written to give a brief overview of a specific chapter in the civil rights movement: the 1961 Freedom Rides and their effect on the state of Alabama in general and its capital city, Montgomery, in particular. It is being published in collaboration with the Alabama Historical Commission to celebrate the 50th anniversary of the Freedom Rides and the opening of a Freedom Rides museum at the old Montgomery Greyhound station.

Most of my work on Alabama and the freedom rides has taken place a block from the site where the Riders were beaten. Being in Montgomery and meeting those involved in the movement, then and now, reminds me that history is never far behind.

Sources, including John Lewis's memoir *Walking with the Wind* and Ann Bausum's *Freedom Riders*, are listed at the back of the book. I'm thankful to Ray Arsenault for his tireless research and for letting us use his roster of freedom riders. Thanks, also, to editor Randall Williams and publisher Suzanne LaRosa for nurturing me and giving me this opportunity to learn about the Riders' extraordinary undertaking, and to NewSouth Books as a publishing house dedicated to promoting cultural understanding.

I am grateful for every one of my friends around the world and especially to my family, with their combination of rigorous thinking and compassion.

We all owe the freedom riders, their predecessors, and those who followed and still follow in their footsteps. It is one thing to notice injustice. It is another thing to care. To act is even rarer.

THE FREEDOM RIDES AND ALABAMA

1

WHY THE FREEDOM RIDES?

The objective of the 1961 Freedom Rides was to travel across the South and integrate transportation facilities. Whites and blacks would ride together and deliberately use either "whites-only" or "colored" facilities, regardless of race. The goal was simple. Its execution and reception was not. Violence as well as subtler forms of discouragement such as bureaucratic opposition and internal conflicts awaited the riders.

The riders' arrival in Alabama on May 14, 1961, and in Montgomery on May 20, 1961, were the key moments in the journey. These were turning points for the Freedom Rides, for the state of Alabama, the cities of Anniston, Birmingham, and Montgomery, and the civil rights movement.

Yet the rides themselves were built on a series of decisions and acts that had emerged over the past century.

In 1961, the United States was embroiled in the Cold War. America projected itself as a beacon of democracy against the growing shadow of the Soviet Union. In this international ideological struggle, the United States saw itself as representing hope, and the Soviet Union as standing for oppression. But within America's own borders, a centuries-long conflict between freedom and oppression had never really ended.

The year 1961 was the centennial anniversary of the start of the Civil War, which was fought over issues which lingered for years after the armed conflict concluded. As a result of the Civil War, slavery was abolished, the South remained part of the

United States, and, during Reconstruction, African Americans were granted equal rights. But in the following years, Northern whites made a kind of reconciliation with Southern whites that involved eroding the freedoms that African Americans had gained. As Southern whites continued to mourn their loss and to resent federal encroachment, Southern blacks were pushed to the margins of society in law and custom.

Segregation ordinances and rules came to be called "Jim Crow" laws. The term may have been derived from "Jump Jim Crow," a blackface song and dance common in minstrel shows of the nineteenth century. Jim Crow laws segregated the races and allowed local rules and customs to override federal protections extended to blacks after the Civil War. Discrimination against African Americans was not limited to the South, but only in the South was segregation widely and legally enforced.

From *Plessy v. Ferguson* to *Irene Morgan v. Virginia*

Transportation in the South, like almost everything else, was segregated based on the concept of white supremacy. In practice, this meant that blacks were always relegated to second-class status or treatment or were barred altogether from enjoying goods, services, privileges, and rights available to whites. The Freedom Riders of 1947 and 1961 were following in a long tradition of protest against these injustices.

Prominent nineteenth-century black leaders like Frederick Douglass had protested segregated train seating. Sojourner Truth once got a conductor fired for striking her when she refused to move to a second-class seat. In the 1880s, following enactment of Louisiana's Separate Car Act, the biracial Citizens' Committee to Test the Constitutionality of the Separate Car Law set the earliest precedent for the Freedom Rides of the next century.

On June 7, 1882, Homer Plessy, an "octoroon" (one-eighth African), was arrested on a train when he remained seated in the whites-only section. In a state court trial, the ruling was that states had the right to regulate transit within their borders. Citizens' Committee's attorney Albion Tourgee appealed to federal courts and argued that Plessy's Fourteenth Amendment rights had been violated. On May 18, 1896, the United States Supreme Court ruled against Plessy. Justice Henry Billings Brown wrote the majority opinion that separate but equal facilities did not contradict equal rights as outlined in the Fourteenth Amendment.

In a solo dissent, Justice John Harlan stated, "Our Constitution is color-blind ... In respect of civil rights, all citizens are equal before the law." He correctly predicted that this decision would inspire "brutal and irritating" aggressions against African American rights and encourage states "to defeat the beneficent purposes which the people of the United States had in view when they adopted the recent amendments of the Constitution." Harlan foresaw that the *Plessy* doctrine of "separate but equal" would be applied throughout the South to schools, hospitals, parks, and every public service imaginable.

The legal issue of segregated transportation was revisited half a century later when Virginia authorities arrested factory worker Irene Morgan for not giving up her seat on a bus. A deputy grabbed her. Recovering from a miscarriage, she kicked him "where it would hurt a man the most."

The National Association for the Advancement of Colored People (NAACP) appealed Morgan's arrest and conviction. Happily, the United States was in a different place in 1946—after two world wars in which black soldiers had fought for the U.S.—than it was when Homer Plessy was arrested in 1882. This time, the Supreme Court declared segregated seating on interstate transportation to be unconstitutional.

Truman Executive Order Desegregates the Military

In 1947, President Harry Truman's Committee on Civil Rights

recommended ending discrimination in the military. Truman, who was the first president to address an NAACP convention, took the suggestion to heart. He proposed a series of civil rights acts, including the desegregation of the military. Horrified by stories of lynchings, he included an antilynching law. Fellow Democrats, or "Dixiecrats," as Southern Democrats were called, opposed his plans. On the other hand, labor leader A. Philip Randolph warned that African Americans would boycott the military if it weren't desegregated. Truman was also struggling with the beginnings of the Cold War.

Truman's solution was to back away from his legislation and instead issue Executive Order 9981, which expanded on President Franklin D. Roosevelt's Fair Employment Act. Truman's order directly ended segregation in the military: "It is hereby declared to be the policy of the President that there shall be equality of treatment and opportunity for all persons in the armed services without regard to race, color, religion, or national origin." Truman's bold move towards equality stunned both supporters and opponents.

The city of Montgomery was particularly piqued by this order. Its two Air Force bases, Maxwell and Gunter, provided the city with tens of millions of federal dollars. Truman's order was a reminder that Montgomery had lost its standing since the Civil War and was now dependent on federal money for support.

But the military had to comply, even within the South.

The 1947 Journey of Reconciliation

The Irene Morgan decision was largely ignored in the South. Transportation officials used technicalities to maintain segregation by pointing to private "company rules" instead of state law.

Some African Americans protested, with mixed results. World War II veteran Wilson Head rode at the front of a bus from Atlanta to Washington. Black historian John Hope Franklin accidentally sat in the wrong seat after donating blood to his dying veteran brother. When told to move, Franklin refused, and other blacks on the bus encouraged him. Both he and Head braved intimidation, but neither were arrested or attacked.

Veteran Isaac Woodard suffered a more horrific fate on a trip in South Carolina. A bus driver swore at him when he asked to use the restroom at a stop, and Woodard swore back. At a subsequent stop, the driver complained to police, who attacked Woodard with a billy club. After fighting in the Pacific for more than a year, Woodard had returned home only to be beaten so severely that he lost his sight. In spite of army doctors' testimony and an FBI investigation, an all-white jury in Columbia, South Carolina, acquitted the police chief involved.

Meanwhile, President Harry Truman's creation of a Commission on Civil Rights had given activists hope. The Fellowship of Reconciliation (FOR), founded by Christian pacifists in 1914, favored direct action. Inspired by Gandhi's nonviolent struggles against colonialism, FOR's Racial-Industrial Department secretaries Bayard Rustin and George Houser contemplated an interracial bus ride.

Neither had much experience in the South. Born in West Chester, Pennsylvania, Rustin had attended school in Ohio—where he was expelled for his homosexuality and for challenging authority—and Pennsylvania before moving to Harlem during the Great Depression.

Inspired by his Quaker grandmother, Rustin turned his talents (he was a brilliant student, singer, and athlete) towards promoting communism and eventually socialism. He thought nonviolence was the solution to the black struggle due to African Americans' adaptability, endurance, and faith. Rustin protested injustices during his three years in prison for draft evasion, and when released he traveled across the United States for FOR practicing civil disobedience and preaching pacifism. He was arrested and beaten

A Library of Congress photo depicting a typical segregated bus depot waiting room in the Jim Crow era.

for refusing to move to the back of a bus in Nashville.

In 1942, Rustin, Houser, Homer Jack, and James Farmer founded the interracial Chicago Committee of Racial Equality, later renamed Congress of Racial Equality (CORE). Farmer was born to intellectual, well-educated parents in Marshall, Texas. He watched his multilingual father defer to whites and experienced Southern segregation first hand when he had difficulties finding food, shelter, and restrooms during his travels.

At the Howard University School of Theology, Farmer was introduced to Gandhianism. Instead of becoming a Methodist minister, he contributed his powerful elocution skills to FOR. Farmer loved the idea of the proposed ride but was unable to participate. (He ended up leaving FOR and CORE, but he would return to CORE as its national director in time to spark the Freedom Rides of 1961.)

Rustin and Houser hoped that their FOR-sponsored ride, which they named the Journey of Reconciliation, would expose CORE to the South, increasing funds and improving knowledge about the national civil rights movement. They listened to warnings from Southern contacts to avoid the deep South. The NAACP did not support the idea. Attorney Thurgood Marshall, who eventually became the first African American to serve on the Supreme Court, thought the idea was well-meaning but dangerous. Rustin argued that violence was inevitable, but using nonviolence would keep bloodshed to a minimum. He and Houser quietly scoped out the journey, researching Jim Crow laws and conferring with activists about housing. This step helped convince NAACP, but tensions remained. CORE sought to enforce NAACP's legal groundwork through direct action, but NAACP's focus remained on legal means.

Despite objections by women who had helped plan the trip, CORE decided a mixed-sex group would exacerbate problems. They had difficulty finding eight white men and eight black men with enough time and dedication to take the trip. Ultimately, fewer than half finished the whole journey, and they had to draw on CORE activists to complete the group. CORE members joining the trip included Rustin, Houser, founder and Unitarian minister Homer Jack, biologist Worth Randle, law student Andrew Johnson, pacifist lecturer Wallace Nelson, social worker Nathan Wright, and chief publicist James Peck.

James Peck would become the only person to take part in both the Journey of Reconciliation and the 1961 Freedom Rides. A radical from his youth, he had brought a black date to his Harvard freshman dance, offending both his wealthy Manhattan family and the school. Alienated for his political beliefs and background in Judaism (his family had converted to Episcopalianism), Peck dropped out and moved to Paris. When he returned to the United States, he founded the National Maritime Union and befriended

American Civil Liberties Union founder Roger Baldwin. Before joining CORE, Peck went to prison for draft evasion (one of six riders to have been conscientious objectors). There he desegregated the prison mess hall by leading a strike.

Also traveling on the Journey were FOR Methodist ministers Louis Adams and Ernest Bromley from North Carolina, jazz musician Dennis Banks from Chicago, Joseph Felmet with the Southern Workers Defense League from Asheville, North Carolina, civil rights attorney Conrad Lynn from New York City, peace activist Igal Roodenko from upstate New York, North Carolina A&T College agronomy instructor Eugene Stanley from Greensboro, North Carolina, and New York Council for a Permanent FEPC member William Worthy.

None of the young travelers had practiced direct action in the South. Rustin and Houser handed out pamphlets stating that they were establishing U.S. law. The group role-played for two days. Instructions were to remain calm, to not leave the bus unless arrested, to go peacefully if taken away, and to raise bail or have an organization pay.

On April 9, 1947, the riders and two African American journalists set off from Washington, D.C., Greyhound and Trailways stations. They made it to Richmond, Virginia, without difficulty. A few fellow passengers even sat outside their regulated seats. Leigh Avenue Baptist Church welcomed the riders, but middle-class students at the all-black Virginia Union College hardly acknowledged racial discrimination in transportation.

On the trip to Petersburg, a passenger warned that "the farther South you go, the crazier [bus drivers] get." The Greyhound driver called the police when Rustin didn't switch seats after being asked, but the police made no arrests. Most black passengers seemed to approve. The Trailways bus driver told Conrad Lynn to move and didn't listen to his invocation of the *Morgan* ruling. The driver said he followed his employers' rules about segregation, not the Supreme Court's. Others on the bus, black and white, didn't support Lynn, and a policeman hauled him away. Lynn was released on a $25 bond and soon joined the others at St. Augustine's College in Raleigh.

In Durham, North Carolina, a Trailways superintendent told the group that while Greyhound might be letting them ride, Trailways was not. Rustin, Peck, and Andrew Johnson were arrested, and local black leaders encouraged others to shun the troublemakers. However, a rally for the riders gained support, and the NAACP secured their release.

Chapel Hill appeared to be a racially progressive college town. The white Reverend Charles M. Jones housed them, but when boarding a Trailways bus to Greensboro, Joe Felmet, Igal Roodenko, Johnson, Peck, and Rustin were arrested. The driver passed out cards absolving the company from liability. The cards didn't particularly impress other passengers.

After the riders posted bail, a group of cab drivers surrounded Peck. One man struck Peck but walked away, confused, when Peck didn't retaliate. The group almost attacked a white minister and a black teacher who stepped in before realizing that they were from North Carolina.

Carrying sticks and rocks, the taxi drivers followed Jones and the riders to his house. They left without incident, but that night Jones received a phone call threatening to burn down his house. Jones had three university students drive the riders and made sure the police accompanied them to the county line. In the following days, staunch segregationists menaced Jones and other perceived liberals. University of North Carolina at Chapel Hill President Frank Graham put an end to the assaults by insisting on police action.

The Shiloh Baptist Church in Greensboro embraced them as it would eventually embrace the 1961 Freedom Riders. On the leg to Asheville, where riders would stay with Joe Felmet's parents, a white South Carolinian said the riders would have been removed or killed in his state, but one bus driver accepted the *Morgan* explanation and told a frustrated soldier to "kill the bastards up in Washington" instead of rider Wallace Nelson.

In Asheville, Peck and Dennis Banks were arrested. In jail, Peck was threatened by white inmates, while Banks was regarded by a few of the black prisoners as a hero. Their NAACP-affiliated attorney Curtiss Todd became the first black lawyer to practice in an Asheville courtroom, where even Bibles were marked "colored" and "white." The judge hadn't heard of the *Morgan* decision and sentenced Peck and Banks to thirty days on the road gang. Todd paid the $800 bond, and they were released.

The group embarked on their first nighttime ride in Knoxville, Tennessee. Chicago activist Homer Jack found the Southern night foreboding but concluded that their biggest enemies were fear and apathy. They caught the train in Nashville, where the conductor thought Nathan Wright was Jack's prisoner. When set straight, he told them to go to the "Jim Crow coach" and claimed that in Alabama they'd be thrown out the window. They stayed put, and the conductor remained flabbergasted.

After a few more arrests and much more confusion from law enforcers, the Journey of Reconciliation came to an end in Washington on April 23. Arrests were cleared or dropped everywhere except in Chapel Hill, where Rustin, Johnson, Roodenko, and Felmet were sentenced to thirty days on the road gang. The NAACP refused to appeal to the Supreme Court. They claimed to have lost the ticket stubs proving that the defendants were interstate travelers, but NAACP's budget was thin, and its focus was on legal battles over issues such as school desegregation.

Rustin, Felmet, and Roodenko decided to prove their commitment by accepting the sentences. They were released after twenty-two days, with their sentences shortened by a week for "good behavior." Rustin later described in a serialized memoir the prison camps' harsh conditions and the guards' hatred toward "Yankees."

The black press said the journey raised awareness among Southerners about solutions to segregation. Riders assessed that the trip informed passengers and law-enforcement officers, and it proved that direct action could lead to enforcement of the *Morgan* decision.

CORE considered the journey a success and expected more interracial rides, but there were none. In the 1950s, when the country froze under McCarthyism, FOR dwindled and eventually withdrew support from a floundering CORE. The NAACP refused to fund another proposed Ride for Freedom.

The 1961 Freedom Rides would have a very different effect from the largely forgotten Journey of Reconciliation.

2

Advances against Segregation in the 1950s

A significant blow to Jim Crow segregation was struck in 1954 in the landmark lawsuit now known as *Brown v. Board of Education*. That historic ruling by the U.S. Supreme Court overturned the Court's earlier "separate but equal" legal doctrine established with the Plessy case in 1896.

Brown was argued by NAACP lawyers Thurgood Marshall, James Nabrit, and George E. C. Hayes as the consolidation of several cases in which citizens objected to "separate but equal" schooling in Kansas, Delaware, Virginia, South Carolina, and the District of Columbia.

The Supreme Court unanimously agreed with the NAACP's argument that segregation was contrary to a fundamental right to education. Chief Justice Earl Warren stated, "We conclude that, in the field of public education, the doctrine of 'separate but equal' has no place. Separate educational facilities are inherently inequal."

Predictably, reaction from white Southerners and politicians was hostile. A segregationist Birmingham policeman named Theophilus Eugene "Bull" Connor uttered a self-fulfilling prediction that "blood would run in the streets" as a result of school desegregation. Riots and violence followed the ruling, and Southern governors vowed to resist the *Brown* proscriptions. South Carolina Senator Strom Thurmond and nearly one hundred Southern congressmen issued a "Southern Manifesto," signed by representatives from every former Confederate state. The document stated that the

Brown decision "planted hatred and suspicion where there has been heretofore friendship and understanding" between the races. They called the ruling immoral and illegal.

In February 1956, the University of Alabama admitted African American student Autherine Lucy, although she was met by hostile mobs and suspended for her safety (she returned and graduated three decades later). In 1957, President Eisenhower had to send federal troops to Central High School in Little Rock, Arkansas, to control white mobs intent on preventing integration. Several towns—including future Freedom Rides destination Farmville, Virginia—closed their public schools and opened private schools for whites only, ignoring the educational needs of blacks altogether.

Montgomery Bus Boycott and the SCLC

On December 1, 1955, in Montgomery, Alabama, Rosa Parks added her name to the list of those protesting segregated transportation. When a white man waited for her to stand so he could sit on a crowded bus, she stayed put and was arrested. The resulting boycott of Montgomery's city buses by the black community launched young minister Dr. Martin Luther King Jr. into the public eye. He was elected to lead the Montgomery Improvement Association (MIA), the organization created to coordinate the boycott. Two members of the Fellowship of Reconciliation, Glenn Smiley and Bayard Rustin, traveled to Montgomery and advised the MIA on strategy and how to organize the tens of thousands of boycotters. For more than a year, young and old walked or carpooled to the places they needed to go.

Montgomery's white leadership—stuck in "massive resistance" mode—assumed that the black community had neither the fortitude nor the managerial skills to continue the boycott. In early 1956, the local chapter of the White Citizens Council drew an estimated 12,000 whites to a local arena for a rally resolving to

Dr. Martin Luther King Jr. with attorney Fred Gray, Montgomery, 1956.

stand firm on segregation. (The WCC had formed in Mississippi to challenge the *Brown* decision and to fund private white schools; it quickly spread across the Deep South, attracting white businessmen and politicians.) Meanwhile, members of the Ku Klux Klan and other extremists responded to the boycott by bombing homes and churches.

On February 1, 1956, local attorney Fred Gray filed a federal lawsuit challenging the city ordinance requiring segregated seating on Montgomery's city buses. *Browder v. Gayle* was heard by a three-judge federal court panel. Judge Frank M. Johnson Jr., writing for the 2–1 majority, declared that the segregation ordinance was unconstitutional in light of the *Brown* doctrine. In December 1956, the boycott successfully ended and Montgomery's black citizens returned to the city buses free to sit where they pleased.

The bus boycott had lasting and far-reaching significance.

FOR put out a comic book about the event, and Dr. King wrote a memoir, *Stride Toward Freedom*, both of which inspired future freedom riders and frightened Montgomery's white community. After the boycott, fewer whites rode Montgomery buses. Local whites who were considered moderate or "soft" on segregation were ignored or harassed. Staunch segregationists banned African Americans from competing in local sports or using the public library. A 1959 federal ruling forbidding segregation in public parks prompted city leaders to close the parks.

In the aftermath of the boycott, sixty activists and ministers met in Atlanta to organize the Southern Christian Leadership Conference (SCLC). The group elected Martin Luther King Jr. as president and another Montgomery minister, Ralph Abernathy, as treasurer. The SCLC espoused a nonviolent, global dedication to democracy and biracial cooperation.

Civil Rights Acts and President John F. Kennedy

There was reason for hope that segregation was breaking down. In 1955, the Interstate Commerce Commission (ICC) had administratively forbidden segregation in interstate travel. In 1957, President Dwight Eisenhower furthered voting rights by signing a Civil Rights Act, the first civil rights legislation since the nineteenth century.

Eisenhower's signing of the 1960 Civil Rights Act heightened civil rights advocates' expectations. They also found young President John Fitzgerald Kennedy's election promising. Change came slowly, though, and the Kennedy administration apparently viewed the fight for civil rights as a distraction compared to the Cold War threat of the Soviet Union.

Sit-ins, the Nashville Movement, and SNCC

On February 1, 1960, four black college students entered a Woolworth's five-and-dime in Greensboro, North Carolina, and took seats at the traditionally whites-only lunch counter. They were refused service, so the group simply sat and waited. They returned the next day, and their widely publicized persistence inspired immediate and widespread imitations of this new nonviolent form of resistance to Jim Crow segregation. From the Midwest to Atlanta and Montgomery, African American or interracial groups stood or sat at lunch counters or restaurants until everyone was served or there were enough of them to fill the establishment. On that first day in Greensboro, an elderly white lady told the four young black men how proud she was of them and that she wished that they had protested sooner. In many sit-ins, however, participants were arrested by police and attacked by store managers and employees or whites who had gathered to protest the protesters.

Nonetheless, nonviolence was gaining strength as an organizing tactic, particularly in Nashville, Tennessee. There the Reverend James Lawson, a professor at Fisk University, had been quietly providing Nashville students with workshops on Gandhian nonviolence. In 1959, students organized the Nashville Student Movement (NSM). Over the next two years, NSM protested a mayoral speech in front of city hall, performed sit-ins, and campaigned against segregated movie theaters. The NSM participants included future freedom riders John Lewis and Frederick Leonard and Freedom Rides organizer Diane Nash, who said that she began "to feel the power of an idea whose time had come."

Inspired by the NSM's calculated organizing and by the spontaneous Greensboro sit-ins, college students from across the South—mostly from historically black universities—gathered in April 1960 at Shaw University in Raleigh, North Carolina. Out of this conference emerged a new black-led organization, the Student Nonviolent Coordinating Committee (SNCC). The new group (pronounced "Snick") quickly began organizing student protests across the country. The young civil rights activists were supported by their older peers. SCLC gave SNCC $800 in seed money, and

SCLC's Ella Baker attended SNCC's first conference. SNCC would soon play a momentous role in the Freedom Rides.

Boynton v. Virginia

In Richmond, Virginia, Alabama native Bruce Boynton was arrested for using the white restaurant in a Trailways bus station. NAACP attorney Thurgood Marshall represented the Howard University law student. On December 5, 1960, the U.S. Supreme Court sided with Boynton. Justice Hugo Black read the court's decision that interstate passengers could expect service to "be rendered without discrimination, as prohibited in the Interstate Commerce Act." This ruling, the new law of the land under the founding principles of federalism, should have immediately de-segregated bus and train station restrooms, waiting rooms, and restaurants. But, like many decisions of its kind, *Boynton v. Virginia* had little immediate effect in the Jim Crow South. The U.S. courts could pronounce rulings, but enforcement of them had to come from federal, state, and local governments. The Freedom Riders were soon to illuminate that conflict.

3

The 1961 Freedom Rides

C ORE national director James Farmer knew that only
something drastic would make the federal government
overcome its fear of political backlash and enforce its
equal rights laws. He wanted to "make it more dangerous politically for the federal government not to enforce federal law than it
would be for them to enforce federal law." Against the backdrop
of the sit-ins and the new energy of SNCC, Farmer saw an opportunity in the ICC rulings and the *Boynton* decision. He spoke
with CORE executive secretary Marvin Rich about a revival of
the 1947 Journey of Reconciliation. Farmer and Rich thought the
risk of prison time for the participants would raise the stakes even
beyond those of the sit-ins.

They named their concept "Freedom Rides" (there would be
no "reconciliation" this time). The conceived rides would test the
commitment of the Kennedy administration to desegregated
transportation facilities by means of an interracial group that
would travel through the deep South.

In line with Gandhian principles, Farmer wrote letters de-
scribing the Freedom Rides plan to President John F. Kennedy,
his brother Attorney General Robert Kennedy, FBI Director J.
Edgar Hoover, the presidents of the Trailways and Greyhound
bus companies, and the chairman of the ICC. Farmer received
no responses. The only media attention came from two African
American journalists.

CORE sought participants for the rides by advertising in the

SNCC newsletter, *The Student Voice*. Farmer and other CORE staffers read the applicants' essays, recommendations, and, in some cases, parental consent forms, and selected fourteen candidates (three of whom were unable to make it for the scheduled departure).

Retired professor Walter Bergman and his wife Frances were the oldest participants at ages 61 and 57. New England pacifist Albert Bigelow had served as a U.S. Navy captain during World War II, but in 1958 he had protested the use of nuclear weapons by steering a boat into a South Pacific testing zone. Other older members included James Farmer and James Peck (the only veteran of the 1947 Journey of Reconciliation).

Also chosen were CORE field secretaries Joseph Perkins, Genevieve Hughes, and Isaac Reynolds, staffer Ed Blankenheim, former NAACP youth secretary Elton Cox, New York folksinger Jimmy McDonald, and students Robert Griffin, Herman Harris, Ivor "Jerry" Moore, Mae Frances Moultrie, Charles Person, Hank Thomas, and John Lewis.

An Alabamian and a veteran of the Nashville sit-ins, Lewis had been thrilled to read about the Freedom Rides. He had previously written to activist Reverend Fred Shuttlesworth about testing segregated waiting areas at the Birmingham Greyhound station. The fiery Shuttlesworth often defied authority and had tried to enroll his daughter in a white grammar school, but even he didn't think the time was right for that particular action.

In late April 1961, the about-to-be freedom riders gathered in Washington, D.C., at a Quaker-run Fellowship House, where they studied Gandhi's and Thoreau's writings about civil disobedience. James Lawson of Nashville trained them for three days, bringing in social activists to role play with the volunteers. They also met with sociologists and lawyers who described economics, ideologies, and legal rationales in the Deep South.

It was a sober exercise. The eighteen riders knew they might die. Some wrote to loved ones and drew up wills.

On May 4, 1961, six whites and twelve blacks boarded a bus. With the help of organizers Diane Nash and Gordon Carey, they planned to travel through Virginia, North Carolina, South Carolina, Georgia, Alabama, Mississippi, and Louisiana. Their goal was to arrive in New Orleans on May 17, the seventh anniversary of the 1954 *Brown v. Board* decision.

Through the Upper South

Farmer's letters must have had some effect, for colored and whites-only signs were temporarily taken down in many of the Virginia stops. The riders passed through Fredericksburg, Richmond, Petersburg, Farmville, Lynchburg, and Danville without incident. The first trouble came in Charlotte, North Carolina, when Joe Perkins went into a Greyhound station barbershop and asked for a shoe-shine, which was denied. He was arrested when he refused to leave, but his case was thrown out in court the next day.

The other riders continued on, and, as expected, the further South they went, the more opposition they met. In Rock Hill, South Carolina, a group of young white men were playing pinball machines and loitering around the station. Two stopped John Lewis from entering a white waiting room. As he had been taught, Lewis cited the *Boynton v. Virginia* decision. They responded by punching him in the face and kicking him.

Genevieve Freeman and Lewis's seatmate Albert Bigelow stepped in to shield Lewis and were attacked as well. A watching police officer finally intervened when the white youths knocked Genevieve Freeman to the ground. When asked by police if he wanted to press charges against his attackers, Lewis said no. The Freedom Riders viewed their white attackers as symptoms of a problem, not the disease itself.

The attack in Rock Hill was overshadowed in the media that day by Alan Shepherd's launch into space on NASA's first manned rocket. The riders quietly made their way to Rock Hill's

Friendship Junior College, home to sit-in veterans who greeted and hosted them.

Then the ride continued. Though the group successfully rode through the rest of South Carolina and into Georgia, several riders left along the way. Elton Cox had to prepare a sermon for Mother's Day, John Lewis departed to be interviewed for a job, and James Farmer left after hearing the devastating news of his father's death.

The riders reached the 700-mile mark in Georgia and dined with Martin Luther King Jr. in Atlanta on Saturday, May 13.

They then decided to split into two groups to test both the Greyhound and Trailways lines. King had his doubts. He privately told a reporter who was covering the event, "You will never make it through Alabama."

4

THE RIDES REACH ALABAMA

B y now, awareness of the rides was spreading and publicity was building. Support for the rides was mixed even within the civil rights community. While speaking at a race-relations conference, Thurgood Marshall said that he felt it was irresponsible and dangerous to continue the Freedom Rides into Alabama and Mississippi. Alabama Governor John Patterson declared there would be no protection for the freedom "rioters" in his state. As they crossed into Alabama, the riders were aware that they were entering a state in which the Ku Klux Klan had significant numbers, including among local leaders and police officers. As they plunged into the Heart of Dixie, signs at the outskirts of small towns greeted them with emblems of the Klan.

Arrival in Anniston

On Sunday morning, May 14—Mother's Day—the Greyhound bus pulled into Anniston, Alabama. A crowd of about two hundred whites met the riders at the station. Local Klan leader Kenneth Adams had read of the riders' impending arrival and had organized a hostile reception. He and Anniston's well-established KKK members were particularly active on Sundays, when they had most of the day off. Many in the mob had come over right from church.

The waiting mob members carried knives, pipes, bricks, and

chains. The bus driver pulled away when the ominous crowd began to throw stones and beat on the sides of the bus. But some in the mob had managed to slash the rear tires of the bus. The mob piled into pickup trucks and cars and followed the bus for six miles until flat tires forced the driver to stop on the side of the road.

The screaming crowd surrounded the bus and pulled at the door. Riders dropped to the ground as rocks and bricks shattered windows. A homemade molotov cocktail came flying inside the bus and quickly set it afire. The riders tried to escape the smoke and fire, but the attackers, who had been trying to get in, now held the door shut. The riders thought they might die in the fire but were equally afraid of being killed by the throng outside.

Finally E. L. Cowling, an undercover State of Alabama investigator who had been traveling with the riders, drew his pistol and pointed it at the whites who were holding the door shut. Cowling's show of force, and the fear that the bus would explode, forced the mob back. Cowling ushered the riders off the bus.

No sooner than the riders had escaped the inferno, the fuel tank did explode. The riders staggered from the blast into the hands of

The fire-bombed bus outside Anniston, Alabama.

AN EDITORIAL

People are asking: 'Where were the police?'

THE CITY OF Birmingham is normally a peaceful, orderly place in which people are safe.

Harrison Salisbury of The New York Times last year came to Birmingham and wrote two articles about us which said, in substance, that "fear and hatred" stalked our streets.

The Birmingham News and others promptly challenged this assertion. The News argues Birmingham people, as others know them, and they didn't fit this definition.

But yesterday, Sunday, May 14, was a day which ought to be burned into Birmingham's conscience.

Fear and hatred did stalk Birmingham's streets yesterday.

Fear and hatred stalked the sidewalks around the Greyhound bus terminal directly across the street from Birmingham's City Hall.

Fear and hatred rode, around in a dozen or more automobiles loaded with men, some of whom may have been from Birmingham, others of whom positively were from other counties. License plates gave them away.

In the whole general area of the City Hall and the Greyhound bus terminal especially, police cars roared, in some number.

Uniformed men were visible. Something was up.

WHAT WAS UP was the advance on Birmingham of a group of Negroes and some whites who gave themselves the title, "Freedom riders."

These people were moving through the South to create racial trouble to make headlines not only here but in every city in the United States and in quite a few foreign capitals.

The Birmingham News has said repeatedly, and it says it again now, that such persons want trouble, that every riot they can bring about, every beating, every arrest, is grist to their mill. They

take deep-seated pleasure in such attacks. It does make headlines. It brings to them more ammunition, money, support for the drive to integrate America forcibly down the line—schools, swimming pools, lunchrooms and restaurants, hotels, buses, residential areas—everything.

And The Birmingham News has said also that in facing this threat, the way to resist to combat such movement, is to figure out what such people want Deep South people to do—and then don't do it.

BUT YESTERDAY hoodlums took over a section of Birmingham. They clustered in small

Turn to Page 4, Column 1

LATE FINAL

The Birmingham News

74TH YEAR—NO. 63   32 Pages—2 Sections   BIRMINGHAM, ALA., MONDAY, MAY 15, 1961   PRICE: 5 CENTS

COOLER — Clearing tonight. Tuesday fair, not so warm.

INTEGRATIONIST GROUP CONTINUING TRIP AFTER BRUTAL BEATINGS HERE

Mob terror hits city on Mothers Day

BY TOM LANKFORD, News staff writer

Mothers Day had passed quietly, happily in Birmingham until the moment the huge, dusty bus arrived at the Trailways depot.

Passersby—the public in general—knew nothing of what was to follow.

JFK meeting with K. now thought likely

BY DOUGLAS B. CORNELL
PALM BEACH, Fla. May 15 (AP)—A Kennedy-Khrushchev conference on corrosive cold-war problems has become a definite possibility. The chances that one will be held, and held soon, are rated currently as 3 to 2.

'Freedom' bus target of Anniston mob

Fired by an incendiary bomb hurled through a rear window, a Greyhound bus carrying seven pro-integration "Freedom Riders" goes up in smoke and flame near Anniston yesterday. The passengers,

fearful of a threatening mob outside, remained on the bus until nearly all were overcome by smoke. When this picture was taken the hand of vigilante whites had been dispersed by the Highway Patrol.

Kennedy says he'll give help

BY CHARLIE GRAINGER, News staff writer

The scene of bloody racial violence threatened to shift to Montgomery late today as a battered group of 19 white and Negro integrationists, attacked by gangs here and at Anniston yesterday, decided to carry their bus trip on to the capital city.

A Montgomery authorities braced for the arrival of the bi-racial group as U. S. Atty. Gen. Robert F. Kennedy in Washington was making a personal effort to send another group on their bus rides through the South to test segregation laws.

Kennedy aides said he had been keeping in telephone contact with Alabama officials "and others" today. They said he had also talked on the phone with some members of the integration group here.

An FBI investigation has already begun of two incidents of mob violence in Alabama yesterday.

More stories and photos, Pages 10, 24

Turn to Page 4, Column 1

Inside The News

Tribute to a hero

First of a series of three articles on the life of Gary Cooper is on Page 32

Racial fighting erupts at Trailways station

This was one of the scenes Mothers Day at the Birmingham Trailways bus Depot, as a group of 20 strong attacked both a busload of integrationists called the "Freedom Riders" and bystanders who cried down scenes a barrage of blows and kicks in Jasper & Park of New York City. In the dark scene are reportedly a leader of the group. Some other

persons were injured in the fighting, including a Birmingham Post Herald photographer and a WAPI newsman. Those attacking Peck are unidentified, but the faces of many of them are plainly shown. They are identifiable. Note the man in the dark coat with a raised length of pipe.

Connor statement:

Trouble blamed on out-of-towners

Birmingham Police Commissioner Eugene "Bull" Connor made the following statement on mob violence in Birmingham Sunday:

"I report very much this incident and to happen in Birmingham.

"I have said for the last 20 years that these out-of-town meddlers were going to cause bloodshed if they kept meddling in the South's business.

"These reports from our policemen is a series that both sides were from out-of-town—the men who got whipped and the ones who did the whipping.

"IT HAPPENED on a Sunday, Mothers Day, when we try to let all as many of our policemen as possible as they can spend Mothers Day at home with their families. We got the police to the bus station as quick as we possibly could.

"As I have said before on numerous occasions, we are not going to stand for this in Birmingham. And if necessary we will jail the jail full—and we don't care whom you say or stick on.

"I am saying such to these satellites from out of my city the bone being the man to do is to stay out if they don't want to get slapped in jail.

"Our people in Birmingham are a peaceful people and we invite here any foreign-born people come into our city looking for trouble. And I'd drive just about as far as I can to keep trouble who won't able to find it."

the mob. One man asked a rider if he was okay, and when he said yes, then began assaulting him. Twelve riders were suffering from smoke inhalation, and most bore cuts from the shattered glass. Still, the mob attacked, hitting Henry Thomas with a baseball bat and splitting Genevieve Hughes's lip. One young observer described the scene as "hell."

Miraculously, Fred Shuttlesworth showed up from Birmingham at the head of a fifteen-car caravan carrying armed black men. They whisked the riders away and sought medical help, but all except the white Hughes were denied hospital treatment. Hank Thomas had to be flown to New Orleans for medical care. When Alabama state troopers eventually arrived at the scene of the mob attack and drew their weapons, they made no arrests.

The trailing Trailways bus entered Anniston an hour later. Its arrival has been overshadowed by the famous photos of the burning Greyhound bus, but its reception was no less horrible. No police intervened when eight young white men boarded the bus and beat the riders with clubs and soft drink bottles. The attackers threw Jim Peck, Charles Person, and Walter Bergman to the back of the bus and stomped on Bergman until he lost consciousness.

The assailants' fury spent, they left, and somehow the bus managed to get back on the road toward Birmingham.

Arrival in Birmingham

The Birmingham police were expecting the riders. The police prepared by updating the Ku Klux Klan and agreeing to give them time alone with the riders. Once again, a KKK-led crowd greeted the beleaguered Trailways bus. Its passengers stepped off the bus to be attacked this time by a Birmingham mob.

This crowd assaulted riders and bystanders alike with whatever they could get their hands on, including key rings and chains. Someone snatched and smashed a *Birmingham Post-Herald* photographer's camera before clubbing the photographer with a bat.

A group kicked in CBS radio reporter Howard K. Smith's car windows, ripped his microphone from the dashboard, and dragged him from his car into the street.

They attacked the already beaten Charles Person and Jim Peck, breaking Peck's teeth and pummeling his face into a "bloody, red pulp" in need of 53 stitches, according to Smith. Walter Bergman, also not yet recovered from the attack in Anniston, was again knocked to the ground and repeatedly hit. Ten days later, Bergman suffered a stroke. He lived with brain damage and could not walk for the rest of his life.

After a long fifteen minutes, the police arrived and made a few arrests (although no one was ever convicted). Birmingham Public Safety Commissioner Eugene "Bull" Connor stated that the "trouble-makers" weren't protected because it was Mother's Day and all police officers had been visiting their "mommas." He had supposedly watched the whole scene from his window.

For the second time that day, Fred Shuttlesworth came to the aid of those who couldn't make it to the hospital. He brought the riders to his house and said, "When white men and black men are beaten up together, the day is coming when they will walk together."

Publicity

Photographs of the Anniston bus burning spread instantly throughout the world. One of the photos superimposed onto the Statue of Liberty's torch became the symbol for the Freedom Rides. The images disturbed African diplomats as well as other international contacts. This was President Kennedy's first significant racial crisis, and it was not the kind of negative publicity the U.S. needed in the midst of tense negotiations with the Soviet Union over nuclear arms.

The president consulted with Attorney General Robert Kennedy and Burke Marshall, head of the U.S. Justice Department's

Civil Rights Division. Robert Kennedy urged the riders to give up their journey, but he sent a personal representative, John Seigenthaler of Nashville, to be with the riders in Birmingham. The attorney general gave Shuttlesworth his personal phone number and told him, "If you can't get me at my office, just call me at the White House."

Southern newspapers were unsympathetic to the riders. The Montgomery paper was amongst a few to condemn the police's absence in Birmingham, mainly because they failed to protect "native white Alabamians against riot and violence." Some letters to the editor congratulated and thanked the attackers, and Alabama congressman George Huddleston Jr. contradicted his statement, "Every decent Southerner deplores violence," by saying that, "these trespassers—these self-appointed merchants of racial-hatred—got just what they deserved."

Meanwhile, James Farmer came to Birmingham from his father's funeral. The riders continued to face resistance, from taunting police officers to menacing mobs. Bus drivers refused to take them out of the city. Restaurants wouldn't serve them food. Many riders should have been in bed recovering. They mulled over their few options. Exhausted, they chose to fly to New Orleans with Seigenthaler.

Getting out of the New Orleans airport was another ordeal. A line of white policemen verbally assaulted the riders until an irritated Seigenthaler told them that he was a Justice Department official.

The riders were disappointed that they had to cancel their journey, but they were relieved to see a band of equally grateful CORE volunteers waiting to take them home. Several riders were unable to hold back tears as they fell into their comrades' arms.

Reinforcements

Upon returning to Nashville from his job interview, John Lewis followed the news of the attacks and the rides' cancellation. In his mind, stopping the rides contradicted the principles of nonviolence. "Truth cannot be abandoned," he later wrote, "even in the face of pain and injury, even in the face of death."

Diane Nash agreed that it was more dangerous to stop than to continue and declared, "If they stop us with violence, the movement is dead." She compared the situation to molding metal, a substance most manipulative when hot and most difficult to shape when cool.

Nash gained support from James Lawson, who wanted to join them in Nashville, and called Jim Farmer to ask for approval for the Nashville Student Movement to take over from CORE. Farmer agreed, despite predicting that continuing through Alabama would be a suicidal "massacre."

Lewis, Nash, and other sit-in veterans paid for the trip to Birmingham with money from the sit-in treasury, but they were short on funds. In spite of worries about continuing the Freedom Rides, older members of the Nashville Christian Leadership Conference (NCLC) gave them $900.

Of the group of students chosen by acting head of NSM's Central Committee James Bevel to revive the Freedom Rides, John Lewis was elected leader. Other riders included: William Barbee, Paul Brooks, Catherine Burks, Carl Bush, Charles Butler, Joseph Carter, Lucretia Collins, Rudolph Graham, William Harbour, Susan Hermann, Patricia Jenkins, Bernard Lafayette, Frederick Leonard, Salynn McCollum, William Mitchell, Etta Simpson, Ruby Doris Smith, Susan Wilbur, and James Zwerg.

Four were white, six were women, and the oldest was twenty-two years old. Most attended Tennessee State University or American Baptist Theological Seminary.

They were heading for Birmingham.

Diane Nash called Fred Shuttlesworth to alert him of their arrival. Because they were quite sure Shuttlesworth's phones were tapped, they used a code which specified race, sex, and number of volunteers. She told him that a shipment of "chickens" was to leave Nashville at dawn the next day.

The reinforcement riders prepared for the worst. Lewis did not even tell his family. James Zwerg, raised in a white, middle class family in Wisconsin, phoned his parents before leaving. They begged him not to go. His mother mentioned his father's weak heart. Zwerg said he had to go. The last thing she said before hanging up was that Zwerg had killed his father.

This second wave of freedom riders left Nashville on the day Lewis had expected to arrive in New Orleans, the anniversary of *Brown v. Board*. The ride to Birmingham was peaceful. Riders were unaware that adversaries knew about their journey. Greyhound employees conferred with one another, some swearing they wouldn't chauffeur "niggers."

Hundreds of policemen and protesters awaited them at the Birmingham Greyhound station. Officers waved them over and boarded the bus. One asked for their tickets and chuckled when he realized who they were. The officer told them that they were breaking the law. Lewis said that they had a right to see friends in the city, but the policeman pushed Lewis into his seat with a billy club, and told him to "sit down and stay there."

The riders had been trained to break down barriers through conversation, but the police didn't respond. They taped newspapers over the windows to prevent the crowd from seeing in, and the riders sat in dark silence for three hours as the crowd grew rowdier.

The police finally cleared a path through the crowd, allowing the riders to get off the bus and make it to the station where Fred Shuttlesworth and Salynn McCollum were waiting. (McCollum was one of the selected students, but she had missed the bus and made it to Birmingham on her own.) Because of this, the police had not identified her, and she was able to call Diane Nash with updates on the situation. Restaurants were closed, so black riders used whites-only restrooms and whites used black restrooms. The next bus for Montgomery was to leave at 5 p.m. Riders sang to pass the time.

The riders easily recognized Bull Connor when he walked in the room. He put the riders under "protective custody" and arrested Shuttlesworth when he tried to interfere. Connor threw the riders into a paddy wagon that took them to jail. McCollum was soon released to her father who took her back to Buffalo, but her role in the Civil Rights movement was hardly done. She would work in Atlanta for SNCC from 1962 to 1963.

The riders couldn't sleep (they were given no mattresses) and fasted for the next two days. They signaled their safety to one another by singing. This expression of freedom disturbed the guards. Connor found it particularly unbearable. Guards threw Zwerg in with white prisoners and hoped to incite them by saying he was a "nigger-lover." Zwerg ended up befriending the drunks and vagrants in his cell, who helped him communicate with other riders.

At 11:30 p.m. on May 18, Connor dropped by to collect seven riders, including Lewis. Completely ignorant of where they were about to go but unwilling to physically fight, the riders went limp and forced the police to drag them. They were placed in unmarked police station wagons.

Connor tried to chat with them. The threat of lynching hung in the air, but Catherine Burks invited him to breakfast and said, "You ought to get to know us better." Connor replied that it would be a pleasure.

Connor put the riders out in Ardmore, on the deserted Tennessee border. The police unloaded the riders' luggage as Connor told them to catch a train "or a bus," he joked, to Nashville, "where they belonged." He chuckled when Burks said, "We'll be back in Birmingham by the end of the day."

There were no streetlights. Riders found their way by moonlight.

The area seemed too central to be a black part of town, meaning it was probably Klan territory. They walked for about a mile and crossed a set of railroad tracks before feeling safe enough to knock on someone's door.

An elderly black man answered. Startled to see seven young men and women carrying suitcases, he apologized for not being able to help them. His wife came to the door, looked at the riders, and convinced him to change his mind. They brought them warm water, and he bought food from several different stores, so as not to raise suspicions by buying large quantities of food at one place. The riders called Diane Nash who immediately sent a Nashville student to pick them up and return them to Birmingham.

The car arrived by mid-morning. Four riders squeezed into the back and three crouched next to the driver. Despite the stifling heat, they felt safer with the windows rolled up. They were amused by a radio announcement claiming the riders were on Nashville's campus, but soon United Press International reported that they were on their way back to Birmingham.

They arrived in Birmingham soaked in sweat but safe. Shuttlesworth provided them with lunch at his place, where they shared chicken and sandwiches with ministers from the Alabama Christian Movement for Human Rights. Shuttlesworth drove them back to the station to meet their fellow riders including Jim Zwerg and Paul Brooks. That morning, a judge had dismissed charges against Zwerg and Brooks and told them to leave town.

Twenty-one freedom riders passed through reporters, police, and a crowd of 3,000 to reach the Greyhound bus set to leave at 3:00 in the afternoon. The bus sat there open and idling, but the driver was nowhere in sight. Someone told them the bus had been cancelled. The riders walked back to the terminal, passing by the same jeering crowd, who poured drinks on them and stepped on their feet. They sat on benches and sang "We Shall Overcome" until they were informed that the 5:00 bus had also been cancelled.

Once political allies, Alabama Governor John Patterson, left, and U.S. Attorney General Robert Kennedy, right, clashed repeatedly over protecting the Freedom Riders.

The riders were prepared to wait for days. Phones had been cut off, restaurants were closed, and sleeping was difficult. Police attempted to restrain the mob with dogs, but a crowd hurled bricks and rocks through the windows, and white-robed KKK members wandered the depot.

Behind the Scenes

Governor Patterson had been speaking with the Kennedys about the Freedom Rides. Patterson said that he couldn't "act as nursemaids to agitators" and stopped responding to the White House's calls.

John Seigenthaler visited Patterson upon leaving New Orleans. Patterson told Seigenthaler that since "the citizens of the state" were so enraged, there was no way to "guarantee the safety of fools." Patterson cited states' rights and professed to be more popular in the country than President Kennedy because he didn't back down to "the goddamned niggers." Seigenthaler knew that the Justice Department would have to take over if Alabama failed to protect the riders.

Seigenthaler himself felt frustrated as he tried to track down the freedom riders. When he found Nash, he told her that if they continued through Alabama all hell would break loose and people would die. She replied, "Then others will follow them."

Federal authorities, bus companies, and local and state officials argued throughout the night. Robert Kennedy famously called the manager of Greyhound's Birmingham terminal and told him to "get in touch with Mr. Greyhound" if he couldn't find a driver.

Riders were told at dawn on Saturday morning that a bus was ready, but unfortunately the assigned driver said, "I have one life to give and I'm not going to give it to CORE or the NAACP," before storming away. (Lewis was impressed that he even knew what CORE was.) Greyhound officials, leaders of local bus drivers' unions, and Bull Connor met with the driver in a back room. They determined that the riders required a heavy escort. At 8:30 a.m., the bus driver returned, the freedom riders boarded the bus, and on that day, May 20, they headed to Montgomery, the Cradle of the Confederacy.

5

Montgomery

As the riders were stuck in Birmingham awaiting a bus to Montgomery, Governor Patterson had stated, "We are not going to escort those agitators. We stand firm on that position." After a night of swearing and shouting, he and Robert Kennedy came to an agreement. Patterson had been one of the few Deep South governors to support John Kennedy's presidential bid in 1960, but that political relationship was now ruined. However, Patterson promised to keep the riders safe. Robert Kennedy sent Seigenthaler and John Doar, the assistant attorney general for civil rights, to supervise the protection. City of Montgomery Police and Public Safety Commissioner L. B. Sullivan and acting Police Chief Marvin Stanley told Patterson, Alabama Public Safety Director Floyd Mann, and the FBI that a group of policemen would await the riders' arrival in Montgomery.

Birmingham police escorted the riders until their bus passed outside the city limits. There the Alabama Highway Patrol, under the direction of Floyd Mann, took over. State trooper cars were stationed every fifteen miles along U.S. Highway 31 the ninety miles between Birmingham and Montgomery. The bus was flanked by motorcycle troopers and cars with news reporters. A small surveillance plane flew overhead.

Sirens blared and lights flashed as the bus sped down Highway 31, but inside the drive was relaxed and even pleasant. Few spoke. The riders assumed they were finally inside the protection of law enforcement.

But as the riders entered Montgomery, the state trooper escort peeled away so the Montgomery police could take over. But they were nowhere to be seen.

Arrival at the Montgomery Station

The Greyhound bus proceeded uneventfully into downtown Montgomery. William Barbee had driven ahead separately and was waiting at the station. Meanwhile, John Seigenthaler and John Doar had stopped for gas, coffee, and a leisurely breakfast. They expected the riders to arrive around 11 a.m. because state officials had assured the Justice Department that the bus would make its usual stops. Unbeknownst to the two Justice Department officials, the bus had sailed past all other Greyhound stations south of Birmingham.

At 10:23 a.m., the bus arrived at the Montgomery station at 210 South Court Street, the driver opened the doors, and the twenty freedom riders disembarked. The scene was eerily quiet and the station was almost deserted. A group of reporters stood on the platform, and a dozen white men stood near the terminal door. A few taxis were parked along the street. John Lewis remarked to William Harbour that the situation didn't feel right.

NBC cameraman Moe Levy stepped towards Catherine Burks and *Life* magazine reporter Norm Ritter asked Lewis a question. Lewis didn't have time to respond. When Ritter saw Lewis's expression, he turned around to see about two hundred white men, women, and children pour out of nearby buildings and alleys. Like the mobs in Anniston and Birmingham, this crowd carried makeshift weapons including hoes, rakes, hammers, ax handles, boards, bricks, chains, sticks, whips, tire irons, baseball bats, ropes, rubber hoses, hammers, and heavy purses.

The journalists, including *Time* magazine correspondent Calvin Trillin, were the first to be attacked. Few photos of the melee survived. A Klan member (who turned out to be an off-duty police officer) clenched a cigar in his teeth as he beat Moe Levy with his own camera and kicked him in the stomach. *Life* photographer Don Urbock's camera was ripped off his neck and smashed into his face.

A middle-aged white woman stirred up the crowd by repeatedly shouting, "Get them niggers!" Another voice yelled that Montgomery would never be integrated. The crowd screamed that the whites were "nigger-lovers" and hurled accusations of communism.

Backed up against a wall, Lewis said, "Stand together. Don't run. Just stand together!" He and the other black riders tried to protect the white riders, but Jim Zwerg was pulled into the mob. Zwerg said he asked God to be with him and "to forgive them for whatever they might do," and felt the "greatest spiritual connection of his lifetime."

Men beat Zwerg in the mouth with his own briefcase. They shoved him to the ground, trampled on his torso and head, and pulled him up again to pin his hands behind his back and continue the assault. The crowd beat him into unconsciousness, but even then they put Zwerg's head between someone's knees and punched him in the face. Women struck him with bags and held up children to claw his face.

The intense focus on Zwerg gave other riders a chance to escape. Allen Cason, Fred Leonard, and Bernard Lafayette jumped over a retaining wall between the bus station and the adjoining federal courthouse and post office and fell eight feet onto a concrete ramp. They then ran through the back door of the building's basement mail room, startling mail workers.

Lucretia Collins jumped into a taxi and observed the assault on Zwerg until she could no longer watch. The other women also got into the taxi, but the black driver was afraid to let the two white women ride in his cab due to the segregation laws. Catherine Burks told him to move over so she could drive, but he didn't budge. So

Susan Wilbur and Sue Hermann stepped out, allowing the five other women to get away.

Wilbur and Hermann found another cab, also with a black driver, but a white man yanked the driver out of the car and the women were pulled into the mob. At this moment, Seigenthaler was driving around the block. He pulled up to the curb when he caught sight of what he called "an anthill of activity." A skinny white teenage boy posed in a boxing stance was punching Wilbur until she fell on Seigenthaler's fender.

Seigenthaler leapt out of the car, grabbed Wilbur, and yelled for her to get in. Hermann escaped a group of taunting men and pocketbook-wielding women and dived into the backseat. But Wilbur, having no idea who Siegenthaler was, pushed him away and told him this wasn't his fight.

Two white men asked Siegenthaler who he was. When Seigenthaler announced that he was a federal official, a third man hit him in the head with an iron pipe. The mob kicked him under his car's rear bumper, where he lay unconscious and unnoticed for twenty minutes.

John Lewis, who was trapped near Zwerg, had grown up in nearby Troy and was familiar with Montgomery and tried to shout directions to the other riders. The mob rounded on him, ripped his suitcase from his hands, and knocked him out with a wooden Coca-Cola crate.

William Barbee also did not escape. The crowd pushed him to the ground, and stomped on his shoulders and head. Three men held him down, rammed a jagged piece of pipe into his ear, and hit him in the head with a baseball bat.

The crowd spat and screamed, "Hit them! Hit them again!" A local African American bricklayer walked into the mob and said that if they wanted to hit someone, they should hit him. They did.

Fred Leonard described the crowd as "possessed." The usually calm John Doar was by now watching the horrific scene from an overlooking window in the adjacent federal courthouse and was on the phone with the Justice Department's Burke Marshall back in Washington. Doar urgently narrated: "There are fists punching . . . It's terrible . . . There's not a cop in sight . . . It's awful." Huntingdon College student George Waldron heard screams being broadcast live by a local radio station and thought that the mob was killing the riders. A Birmingham-based news reporter said that the "terror" in Birmingham didn't compare to this: "Saturday was hell in Montgomery." Many of those present would long remember the day as an expression of animalistic madness.

Alabama State Public Safety Director Floyd Mann had no jurisdiction inside the city limits, but when he arrived and saw that there were no police present, he called troopers. Though he described himself as a moderate segregationist, Mann said he still believed in enforcing the law.

Mann pushed his way into the grasping crowd, located Lewis and Barbee, and fired his gun in the air. (Other riders, not realizing who Mann was, heard the shots and feared the worst for Barbee and Lewis.) Mann pulled men off Barbee's body and said, "I'll shoot the next man who hits him. Stand back. There'll be no killing here today." He also saved the bricklayer and Birmingham television reporter James Atkins from a man wielding a baseball bat: "One more swing and you're dead." The mob backed away. If not for Mann, Barbee would have died.

Commissioner L. B. Sullivan later stated that he hadn't had enough information about the riders' arrival. He claimed he didn't know what had happened. He said that when he finally arrived he "just saw three men lying in the street." Later, he claimed not to have sent the police because he didn't want to draw a crowd.

However, Sullivan was a member of the White Citizens Council. He had stated, "We have no intention of standing guard for a bunch of trouble-makers coming into our city making trouble."

Following in Bull Connor's footsteps, Sullivan kept Klan leader and former Montgomery reserve policeman Claude Henley updated and agreed to wait for at least half an hour before showing up after the riders' arrival. Some Birmingham Klansmen had joined Henley and local KKK members. Despite calls for help, Sullivan kept his word to Henley.

A short time later, Alabama Attorney General MacDonald Gallion arrived at the station. As a bleeding Lewis regained consciousness and tried to stand, Gallion read to him Judge Walter B. Jones's injunction against the riders, written the previous night as Patterson and Kennedy negotiated over the phone. The injunction forbade "entry into and travel within the state of Alabama and engaging in the so-called 'Freedom Ride' and other acts or conduct calculated to promote breaches of the peace." When he noticed Zwerg, Gallion also read the injunction to his unconscious body.

Lewis spotted Barbee, and they tried to lift Zwerg to his feet. A policeman told them they were free to go, but finding transportation was up to them. Sullivan said that all the whites-only ambulances were "in the repair shop." Lewis put Zwerg in the back of a whites-only cab. The driver grabbed his keys and left. A black taxi driver was willing to take Lewis and Barbee, but the police wouldn't let him take Zwerg. The cabdriver dropped off Barbee at St. Jude's Catholic Hospital in west Montgomery and took Lewis to a local black doctor who shaved and cleaned his injured head.

Floyd Mann realized that Zwerg would never be taken to a hospital by Montgomery police, so he and state patrolman Tommy Giles drove Zwerg to St. Jude's. Zwerg briefly revived in the car. Upon hearing Mann's and Giles's Southern accents, Zwerg assumed he was going to be murdered. After they dropped him off, a nurse heard that a mob was approaching to lynch Zwerg. She sedated him so he would be unconscious in case they succeeded.

Zwerg faded in and out of consciousness for two days. He had cuts, bruises, fractured teeth, abdomen trauma, broken thumbs, a broken nose, a severe concussion, and three cracked vertebrae. He later joked that ambulances were only called in Montgomery after someone died.

Both Zwerg and Barbee, lying one floor below Zwerg in the Negro section of the hospital, swore they would continue the Freedom Rides. Zwerg declared, "Segregation must be stopped. It must be broken down. We're going on to New Orleans no matter what. We're dedicated to this. We'll take hitting. We'll take beating. We're willing to accept death."

An iconic photo of a bloodied Zwerg and Lewis appeared on the front pages of newspapers around the world. Afterwards, Zwerg couldn't remember making the above statement that helped galvanize public support for the freedom riders' cause.

He and other riders paid a steep personal price. Zwerg's mother had a nervous breakdown, and his father suffered a heart attack. He stayed in the hospital until May 25, when the FBI drove him to the airport and his family minister took him home to Appleton, Wisconsin. Zwerg experienced pain for the rest of his life, but he and his parents physically recovered; their relationship took more time.

Barbee was permanently damaged. Never the same person afterwards, years later he killed himself by stepping in front of a bus.

Other riders had hidden in a nearby Presbyterian church or were shielded by the black community. Hermann and Wilbur called the police, who forced them to get on a train back to Nashville. A volunteer picked up Lewis from the doctor's and drove him to the home of the Reverend Solomon Seay Sr. Lewis's coat, shirt, and tie were stained with blood, but he was relieved to find $900 still in his pocket.

Reverend Seay had arrived at the station to find two students,

From left to right: Nashville Freedom Riders Bill Harbour,
Lucretia Collins, Jim Zwerg, Catherine Burks, John Lewis, and
Paul Brooks in Chicago in July 1961. (Courtesy of Bill Harbour)

one white and one black, lying in the street. He thought they were
dead, but the riders had been taught to mimic convulsions so they
would seem dead. He tried to collect some of the riders' scattered
possessions before returning home to welcome the others.

The riders embraced one another and were introduced to members of the Montgomery Improvement Association. Gathering
at Seay's house gave the riders a renewed sense of determination.
Nash wanted to harness this feeling of solidarity. She contacted
Martin Luther King Jr. about getting the SCLC to help her plan
a mass meeting in Montgomery.

The riders cheered when they heard that other activists were
on their way. Jim Lawson, Diane Nash, Fred Shuttlesworth,
James Farmer, and Hank Thomas were flying in from around the
country. Farmer called in CORE members from New Orleans
and Ella Baker sent SCLC members from Atlanta. To Robert
Kennedy's chagrin and the riders' delight, Martin Luther King
was on his way.

Riots Continue

The Sunshine Valley Boys sang on Montgomery's WSFA-TV, "On a Greyhound bound for New Orleans was such a gang you have never seen: In rode the no-good 'Freedom Riders'; just a bunch of trouble-making outsiders." Nash, of course, denied that students caused the violence: "The people who committed violence are responsible for their own actions."

The mob at the station grew. Some one thousand whites rioted on and off for the next two days. They threw suitcases and their contents in the air. People who appeared to be normal citizens in their daily lives danced around bonfires built to burn the freedom riders' possessions, including books, notebooks, toothbrushes, deodorant, and suitcases.

Civil rights lawyer Clifford Durr and his wife Virginia watched from Clifford's law office across the street. The white Durrs had been put under surveillance by the FBI and were shunned by their community for their progressive beliefs.

Virginia Durr sent college student Bob Zellner to find her friend Jessica "Decca" Mitford, a British author who was reporting for *Esquire* magazine. He passed by a sheet of plywood with a brick lodged halfway through it before wading into the crowd and spotting Mitford taking notes in the chaos. After alarming her by mentioning her name, Zellner explained who he was and brought her to safety.

The crowd attacked almost every African American in sight. Some soaked a black teenager in kerosene and set his clothes on fire while others jumped on his companion's leg until it broke. Of those injured, Zwerg and Barbee were the most severely hurt, but five riders were hospitalized and more than twenty people received medical treatment.

At 11:30 a.m., Floyd Mann called in sixty-five highway patrolmen and mounted sheriff deputies. At 1 p.m., more police came, dispersed the crowd with teargas, and made a few arrests. Two of those arrested were liberal whites Anna and Fred Gach, who had intervened in the melee. Even though they were trying to help the riders, they were fined $300 for disorderly conduct.

By 4 p.m., the rioting had subsided, but the police's relative inaction encouraged smaller groups of whites to continue demonstrating nearby. Court Street was empty, except for smoke, a few fires, broken glass, camera pieces, shoes, pieces of clothes, and puddles that looked like "glistening red jelly" but were actually blood.

Robert Kennedy was informed of the attack while he was at a baseball game. He called an emergency meeting and tried unsuccessfully to reach Governor John Patterson. Kennedy called the hospital where Seigenthaler was recovering from his fractured skull and broken ribs. Floyd Mann had made an emotional visit to Seigenthaler's bedside, and Kennedy was relieved to talk to an apologetic Seigenthaler. Robert told him not to worry. He admitted that this conflict between states and federal rights seemed inevitable.

News reports and photographs from that day gave the United States worldwide negative publicity. With the approaching Cold War summit in Vienna, the president couldn't ignore what had happened. At the same time, he knew that if he acted he would have political fallout in an area of the country that had supported him and his party. John Kennedy condemned all involved, including the riders, citizens, and local officials.

The Kennedy brothers were furious that Patterson, a political supporter, had allowed an attack on the riders and the attorney general's representative. After midnight Saturday, Robert Kennedy called Patterson to tell him that there weren't enough policemen to regulate the riots. Patterson blamed Kennedy for the problem and called the Freedom Riders "rabble rousers" and "mobsters." He and Kennedy argued into the wee hours of Sunday morning. Finally, Kennedy said his brother, the president, had no choice but to send in federal marshals. He sent a publicized telegram to Patterson justifying the federal government's actions asserting that the Kennedy administration's involvement was a last resort necessary only because assurances that local law enforcement needed no help had been proven wrong.

Patterson considered the federal intrusion to be unconstitutional. He too worried about political backlash. The governor publicly said Alabama had to protect all human lives, "outside agitators" or not, but it was up to the state to determine how to do it.

Mass Meeting

Meanwhile, a mass meeting in support of the Freedom Riders had been called for 8 p.m. Sunday night at the First Baptist Church pastored by the Reverend Ralph Abernathy on North Ripley Street. Diane Nash and the SCLC's Wyatt Tee Walker arrived Sunday morning. James Bevel and Jim Lawson came later that day. Martin Luther King Jr. canceled a talk in Chicago and flew to Atlanta, writing his speech during the plane ride.

Robert Kennedy knew that protecting King would send an unpopular message to the segregationist white South, but he nevertheless sent fifty federal marshals to escort King from the airport to the church and twelve marshals to escort Fred Shuttlesworth.

King greeted the battered riders in the basement library of the church. After helping King, Abernathy, and Walker plan the mass meeting, Shuttlesworth left to pick up James Farmer, who was flying in from Washington. On Shuttlesworth's way to his car, he was assaulted with small stones and stink bombs. When Shuttlesworth returned later with Farmer, harassing whites rocked his car. By now, a large mob was gathered outside the church.

Shuttlesworth and Farmer managed to escape through the nearby Oakwood Cemetery. Circling back around, Shuttlesworth boldly marched directly into the mob, loudly ordering the rioters to make way. A terrified Farmer, who towered over the much smaller Shuttlesworth, followed in his wake. Farmer later described his surprise that he and Shuttlesworth both were not killed and attributed their safe passage through the mob to the mob's astonishment at Shuttlesworth's audacity.

They had an emotional reunion in the church basement.

By now, the church was filled with 1,500 blacks and a few whites, including Jessica Mitford and a white student, Peter Ackerburg, who would eventually join the Freedom Rides. Also present were reporters from three national television networks, state and local newspapers, the *New York Times*, Associated Press, and United Press International. Worried that the mob would try to break in and attack them, the church members tried to disguise the freedom riders as choir members, but Lewis had an unmistakable white x-shaped bandage across his head.

After dark, the mob outside doubled to about 3,000. Growing in size and aggression, the rioters waved Confederate flags, let out Rebel yells, and smashed car windows. The Durrs had loaned Jessica Mitford their car and advised her to park it several blocks away. Instead, she parked right in front and the mob saw a white woman entering the black church. Naturally, hers was one of the first to be overturned and set on fire. When its gas tank exploded, the congregation inside feared the blast was the start of an all-out attack.

Despite widespread publicity about the mass meeting, authorities were slow to arrive. When they did, marshals kept the rioters across the street, and Floyd Mann's plainclothes patrolmen kept an eye on the situation.

The Reverend Solomon Seay Sr. opened the mass meeting with hymns. He described the inspiring courage of the freedom riders and introduced Diane Nash, sitting in the front row. Her presence was an emotional boost to many of the riders. A few other riders made statements, but since they were fugitives, Seay didn't introduce them by name.

Reverend S. S. Seay Sr.

The crowd gave a standing ovation to Floyd Mann. One mother roused her child and told him to stand up and "thank a white public servant who had done his duty." The atmosphere inside the church bespoke courage and confidence, not fear or panic. However, it was obvious that not everyone in the black community planned to rely on nonviolence. Some people carried pistols and knives.

Outside, the chaos escalated. One group of whites made it past the marshals and banged on the church door. By telephone, King asked Robert Kennedy for help. The marshals in Montgomery were undertrained and underequipped, and federal powers were reluctant to tread on "states' rights," but Kennedy assured him that 400 more federal marshals were on their way from nearby Maxwell Field.

Kennedy asked King to delay further Freedom Rides, and King relayed to Nash and Farmer the attorney general's request for a "cooling-off period." Nash vehemently disagreed, causing Farmer to loudly declare that African Americans had been cooling off for hundreds of years: "If we got any cooler, we'd be in a deep freeze."

Outside, the reinforcement federal marshals arrived in military vehicles and postal trucks. A few were scared to leave their vehicles. With nightsticks and tear gas, they tried to restrain the mob, but angry whites continued to throw rocks and bricks at the church. One brick broke a stained glass window and hit an elderly parishioner. Nurses rushed to attend him and everyone dropped

to the floor. Seay insisted that all children be taken to the basement. A few screamed. Tear gas wafted through the window, but
the congregation continued to sing hymns.

Seay told everyone to stay calm and led in singing, "Love
Lifted Me." He stated, "I want to hear everybody sing and mean
every word of it." John Lewis and other riders joined the rest of
the congregation in singing hymns and freedom songs such as
"We Shall Overcome" and "Ain't Gonna Let Nobody Turn Me
'Round." The singing helped them take their minds off the mob
outside and the stifling heat.

At one point, a few rioters pushed their way into the church.
Marshals raced through the church basement and beat them back
with clubs. By 10 p.m., the marshals reported that they were los-
ing control.

Robert Kennedy asked the Pentagon to set up army units
at Fort Benning, Georgia. He asked Mann for help, but Mann
could do little without Patterson, who was listening in on the
conversation. Mann asked for more marshals, but Maxwell had
no more to send.

Gunshots were being randomly fired into nearby African
American homes. The situation was so dire that King and Abernathy considered giving themselves up to the mob to save the
congregation.

Finally, Governor Patterson declared martial law. Commissioner
Sullivan, other city policemen, and 800 Alabama National Guardsmen replaced the federal marshals. Alabama officials declared that
the state had everything under control and needed no more help
from the federal government.

Many inside the church would have felt safer being protected
by federal troops than by the segregationists who made up most
of the Alabama National Guard. One reverend prayed, "Bless all
those cowards standing outside. Bless that stupid governor of
ours." Wyatt Tee Walker, Ralph Abernathy, and James Farmer

Headlines in the Montgomery Advertiser *on the morning after rioters surrounded the mass meeting at the First Baptist Church.*

made statements. The meeting continued to fulfill Nash's wish to foster a powerful sense of unity.

Then King spoke. He noted that the law could not make him loved but it could keep him from being lynched. King urged nonviolent action against segregation in Alabama and stated, "Alabama will have to face the fact that we are determined to be free. Fear not, we've come too far to turn back." He said, "the South proved it required the federal government to prevent it from plunging into a dark abyss of chaos." He compared the barbarity in Alabama to that in Hilter's Germany. King criticized Governor Patterson for creating "the atmosphere in which violence could thrive." Shuttlesworth also called Patterson the "most guilty man in the state."

As for Patterson, he called Attorney General Robert Kennedy back and yelled, "You've got what you want. You got yourself a fight," foreshadowing the coming decade's struggle among citizens, local authorities, and the federal government. Patterson called the riders communists and said that he couldn't help protect King because he wouldn't listen to the police. Kennedy responded that he wanted to personally hear "a general of the United States Army say he can't protect Martin Luther King." Knowing that Patterson's reluctance to intervene had been politically motivated, Kennedy told him that the physical survival of the people in that church was more important than his and Patterson's political survival. But Patterson heard this as yet another insult.

The Guardsmen had secured the area by midnight. Inside the church, people gathered sleeping children and moved towards the doors. But the doors were blocked and the troops outside faced them with bayonets. Guard officers told King that the state had taken over from the federal government and there was no available transportation; those in the church would have to make it through the mob to get home.

King responded that some of the people needed to leave. National Guard Adjutant General Henry Graham, an avowed segregationist, told King that it was too dangerous. King asked Graham to read to the congregants Patterson's declaration of martial law, condemning "outside agitators" and federal authorities. The gatherers were now under protective custody.

King called Robert Kennedy again. By this time, the attorney general wanted to wash his hands of the situation. He told King and Shuttlesworth that they should thank the federal authorities for saving their lives.

Feeling trapped and angry, the large crowd spent the night inside the First Baptist Church, nervous about the Guard's presence and concerned about what was happening outside.

The church was crowded and hot. Tear gas lingered. Though it was difficult to rest, many were grateful to be alive. Freedom Riders tried to cheer up the gatherers. Children slept in the basement, and the elderly rested on cushioned pews. Many lay on the floor.

Meanwhile, Justice Department officials negotiated with Graham to end the siege. One federal official observed that he felt strange in the Guard's office. Confederate flags were everywhere (it was the centennial of the start of the Civil War), but he didn't see a single American flag. Finally, the Kennedy representative threatened to send federal marshals back to the church. Only then did Graham send trucks and jeeps to the church.

By dawn, the mob had somewhat dispersed, and the National Guard began ferrying the people inside the church to their homes.

Regrouping

Newspapers the next day mentioned the night's chaos, but their main focus was the cooperation among local, state, and federal law enforcement. Others, such as former governor Jim Folsom and the Alabama Press Association, were more critical of Patterson and the state. *Montgomery Advertiser* editor Grover Hall Jr. was unsympathetic to the riders, but he condemned Patterson's hypocrisy.

The federal administration praised Mann, denied that they were about to send in troops, and played up the collaborative elements of the night. State and local officials said otherwise. They wanted federal marshals out of the city.

Federal powers agreed to work with local authorities and let the state charge riders. If evidence turned up against any rioters, federal authorities would make arrests. They did not. From the riders' perspective, the federal government showed little interest in upholding their constitutional rights.

Robert and John Kennedy wanted to get the marshals out of Alabama. They had not performed well. The Kennedys knew they were on very tenuous political ground, likely to lose many Deep South Democrats, but Robert worried about how well the Alabama National Guard would protect riders.

The FBI was not much help. They had arrested the four Klansmen supposedly responsible for the Anniston bus burning, but Director J. Edgar Hoover insisted that the FBI's purpose was to investigate, not to protect. FBI agents had recorded the Montgomery riot (with faulty equipment) without intervening. Hoover decided to investigate those he considered more dangerous than the Klan. According to him, these enemies included possible communist radical Dr. Martin Luther King Jr.

Violence against African Americans in Montgomery had continued until National Guardsmen were deployed, but the riders' arrival was a turning point for the city. Ordinary white citizens in the community distanced themselves from the violence. As Solomon Seay Sr. said, the "better class of white people were beginning to get enough." Businessman Winton M. "Red" Blount spoke out against police inaction and urged white business leaders to formally condemn the violence. Because many whites blamed the black students, A resolution was drawn up that criticized both sides. Eighty-seven out of almost one hundred who were asked signed the petition.

John Doar was also able to get U.S. District Judge Frank M. Johnson Jr. to issue a restraining order against Montgomery Klansmen. This gave hope to NAACP lawyers Fred Gray and Arthur Shores. They and several riders spent Monday in the federal building adjacent to the bus station to lift the previously issued state-court injunction against the riders.

John Lewis was nervous about testifying in court for the first

Judge Frank M. Johnson Jr.

time but hopeful because Judge Johnson had sided with Gray in *Browder v. Gayle*. Johnson asked Lewis why he joined the Freedom Rides. Lewis responded that he wanted to see the law carried out. Though Judge Johnson wondered if continuing the rides was intelligent, he considered Alabama Circuit Judge Walter Jones's injunction "an unconstitutional infringement of federal law."

John Lewis stayed at pharmacist Dr. Richard Harris's house on South Jackson Street for the night. One of King's former neighbors, Harris offered his house to SNCC, CORE, and SCLC members, who gathered there to discuss the future of the Freedom Rides. The younger generation—Diane Nash, John Lewis, and James Bevel—sat on the floor, while Ralph Abernathy, James Farmer, Wyatt Walker, James Lawson, and Dr. King sat on folding chairs.

Farmer later admitted that part of his reason for joining the riders was to reclaim the rides for CORE. Another motivation was to share the spotlight with King. Farmer offended many of the Nashville students when he referred to the rides as CORE's.

The younger riders were also frustrated by King. Encouraged by SNCC advisor Ella Baker, Nash tried to convince King to join the next leg of the Freedom Rides into Mississippi. Wyatt Walker, Ralph Abernathy, and Montgomery SCLC staff member Bernard Lee argued that King was too valuable a leader to join them. Walker pointed out that King was on probation for a traffic citation in Georgia. If arrested, he could be thrown in jail for six months.

Younger riders stated that they too faced legal problems. Thinking of how difficult it was to gain Kennedy's assistance, King reluctantly said no. When pressed, he replied, "I think I should choose the time and place of my Golgotha." This statement came across as hubristic to some of the riders. After speaking privately with King, Walker announced that they would no longer discuss the matter. Students left the room, ridiculing King with the nickname, "De Lawd." Paul Brooks was so upset, he contacted NAACP leader Robert Williams about the meeting. Williams telegrammed King and called him a phony.

The next day, on Tuesday May 23, CORE, SCLC, and SNCC called a press conference in Montgomery. Lewis, Abernathy, Farmer, and King made statements declaring that they would press on to Jackson whether the police would protect them or not. In an emotional statement, King said that no one wanted to be martyrs, but the riders were willing to be. He said that Jim Lawson would hold nonviolent training sessions for anyone who wanted to join. The unfortunate result of this conference was that it made King look like the mastermind behind the Freedom Rides.

When interviewed, James Lawson directed attention back to King. Lawson thought King had a legitimate reason not to go on the rides and felt it was both unwise and against nonviolent philosophy to pressure someone into joining them. Lawson's workshops gave the riders strength for the upcoming days and inspired even those who had already gone through training.

Every Tennessee State student, except for Lucretia Collins, who had fulfilled her requirements, headed back to complete school. Tennessee Governor Buford Ellington had threatened to expel the riders. Diane Nash was prepared. By the time they left, she had already sent for reinforcements.

About thirty riders, including Hank Thomas, flew in and prepared to enter Mississippi. They were all apprehensive. NAACP members Roy Wilkins and Medgar Evers warned that Mississippi was too dangerous for the freedom riders. Robert Kennedy admired the riders' fearlessness, but still wished that they would suspend the rides. But the riders couldn't stop their momentum. They got rid of anything that could be construed as a weapon or drug (such as hair pins or sleeping pills), learned about the legal impediments to their journey (though they were doing nothing illegal), and kept in mind that where they were going, they would have no rights.

The rides had attracted national attention when the Nashville students restarted the rides, but now this strategic plan was becoming an organic entity. Rider Jim Davis said that words Zwerg spoke from his bed moved him to catch a bus to Montgomery. People of all ages, religions, and backgrounds traveled across the country to join the rides. Members from CORE, SNCC, SCLC, and NCLC established the Freedom Ride Coordinating Committee in Atlanta to organize the riders.

John Kennedy told Robert Kennedy to "stop them." John Patterson asked the president to send the agitators home. Mississippi Governor Ross Barnett praised Patterson's resistance and repeated Patterson's request. The American Nazi Party sponsored a "hate bus" from Washington, D.C., to New Orleans. Through it all, the riders would not be moved.

6

Leaving for Mississippi

ississippi Governor Ross Barnett relieved Robert Kennedy and annoyed John Patterson by vowing that his state would not see the violence that had happened in Alabama. Barnett told the attorney general to keep his federal marshals at bay. U.S. Senator James O. Eastland of Mississippi told Kennedy that the riders would be safe—in Mississippi jails. Kennedy wasn't pleased, but, grateful for the riders' physical safety, he felt that the federal government could do nothing about the promised arrests.

On Wednesday, May 24, riders convened in Dr. Harris's kitchen for a breakfast prayer meeting. They wondered if they would even make it out of Montgomery. At 6:15 a.m., Alabama National Guardsmen escorted them to the Trailways station where an antagonistic white crowd was kept in check by plainclothes detectives, FBI agents, and 500 National Guardsmen.

King wanted to support the riders and atone for not joining them. He, his brother A. D. King, and Abernathy walked into the Trailways station and ordered food at the white counter. Black waitresses from the Negro counter served them, thus officially desegregating the station's food service. (Though the next day, Abernathy, Shuttlesworth, Wyatt Tee Walker, Bernard Lee, Yale University chaplain William Sloane Coffin Jr., and another group of riders would be arrested when ordering food at the very same lunch counter.)

Twelve riders stepped aboard the Trailways bus, where they

were joined by Floyd Mann, National Guard riflemen, and a dozen photographers. Lawson, who was chosen to be the spokesperson, shook hands with King through the window. National Guard General Graham stepped on the bus and announced that the journey would be "hazardous." He said that he genuinely wished for their safety.

In spite of the escort convoys stretched behind and in front of them, most of the riders felt uncomfortable and scared. They had heard tales about Mississippi, "the Magnolia state," stories of lynchings and bodies dumped in rivers. There were whispers of snipers, booby traps, and bombs. Riders hid wills, notes, and names of relatives in their clothes.

FBI surveillance, two helicopter spotters, and three U.S. Border Patrol airplanes accompanied the caravan. One thousand Guardsmen were stationed between Montgomery and Mississippi.

The bus passed by Selma's angry crowds. The escorting officials stated that it was too dangerous to stop anywhere. Some riders understood the concern but felt that it contradicted the point of the Freedom Rides which was to "travel freely from place to place." They drove by more fist-shaking crowds, and at one point three cars filled with teenagers wove in and out of the convoy.

Riders spent the trip speaking with reporters and singing. They set Harry Belafonte's tune "The Banana Boat Song" ("Day-O") to words about the Greyhound bus: "Freedom's coming and it won't be long."

A mass of Mississippi Guardsmen and patrolmen met the caravan at the state border. Reports of dynamite held up the bus as Guardsmen searched the woods. After an hour, bus drivers traded places, Mississippi Guardsmen replaced Alabama Guardsmen, and Floyd Mann stepped off. Mississippi National Guard commander G. V. "Sonny" Montgomery (later a congressman) got on.

There was no bathroom on the bus. The Reverend C. T. Vivian, who hadn't even consulted his wife before leaving from Nashville for Montgomery, protested having no rest stops along the 258-mile journey. Montgomery's terse dismissal of the concern bothered the riders.

Meanwhile, back in Montgomery, some 2,000 whites mobbed the Greyhound station and threw bottles and rocks at John Lewis, Hank Thomas, and others as they boarded a second bus. James Farmer hadn't planned to continue from Montgomery to Jackson. He helped others load luggage before waving goodbye from the platform. Seventeen-year-old CORE volunteer Doris Castle asked through the window, "Jim, you're going with us, aren't you?" He mumbled something about CORE paperwork and obligations. She stared and said, "Jim, please." Farmer put his luggage on the bus and climbed aboard.

The second bus caught authorities off guard. Troops were still stationed on the road, but the second bus didn't have the same kind of escort. The riders made it out of the station at 11:25 a.m. The ride was tense and uncertain. Journalists were scared away by rumors of ambushes. Only one reporter thought the chance of a good story was worth the risk.

Lucretia Collins, elected leader of the Greyhound group, helped keep everyone on the bus calm by conducting nonviolent workshops and singing. Hank Thomas added a verse to the song, "Hallelujah, I'm a traveling, hallelujah, ain't it fine? Hallelujah... I'm a traveling down freedom's main line." He sang, "I'm taking a ride on the Greyhound bus line, I'm riding the front seat to Jackson this time." They were also comforted by thoughts of the other riders on their way to Jackson.

Mississippi Governor Ross Barnett had told Jackson residents to stay at home. Officials would handle the riders' arrival according to state law and protect riders from mob violence. They would simply arrest them.

Jackson and Mississippi Jails

When the first bus arrived in Jackson, a crowd of journalists and plainclothesmen parted to let the riders walk to the white waiting room. A policeman stopped them there and told them to move along. C. T. Vivian had gone unnoticed into the men's room and was only arrested because he told the police captain that he was with the others.

In the patrol wagon, riders sang "We Shall Overcome," but the journey and arrests had taken a psychological toll. Rider Dave Dennis said that they were all so prepared for death in Mississippi, several freedom riders suffered breakdowns when they weren't met with violence. Some screamed, pulled their hair, and banged their heads against the wall.

When the second bus arrived, the riders were similarly arrested. Farmer mentioned the *Boynton* Supreme Court decision and was immediately arrested. Lewis was arrested while he was at a white urinal.

As the Mississippi jails filled with freedom riders, Robert Kennedy met with SNCC and CORE leaders, including Diane Nash and Charles Sherrod, and advised them to shift their attention to registering voters.

The media was less interested in the Mississippi arrests than it had been in the more sensational violence in Alabama. Attention dwindled, and about two-thirds of the public condemned the riders' goals. Even many who agreed with their ideas disapproved of their methods. In June, *U.S. News & World Report* would state, "The leaders preach 'nonviolence.'. . . Violence, however, has been the result."

The riders went to court two days after their arrests. The judge fined each rider who had been arrested $200 and sentenced them to sixty days in jail for "disturbing the peace," a charge harder to challenge in court than that of violating local segregation laws. The riders refused bail and planned to stay in prison for forty days, which was long enough to cost the state money but to still be able to file an appeal. This was a daunting commitment, especially for the newest riders who had gone through the shortest training session.

In jail, the riders persisted in singing their freedom songs. The violent criminals upstairs heard their voices and traded candy and knickknacks with them. Three days after their arrests, twenty-seven riders were moved to Hinds County Jail, which had fewer amenities and no soap or towels, before being transferred to the Hinds County Prison Farm.

The farm's cells were small. Because of a shortage of beds, some prisoners slept on benches, tables, and floors. They weren't taken out to work with the regular inmates but instead swept and mopped their rooms. Jailers took away smokers' cigarettes and cut out afternoon snacks. Riders were served burnt black coffee in tin cups. After a hunger strike, they began to eat the jail food which consisted of tough meat, biscuits, and syrup.

Superintendent Max Thomas beat C. T. Vivian, Hank Thomas, and Jean Thompson in the head for failing to call him "sir." Jim Bevel kept spirits up with sermons and songs. Still, tensions broke out between the religious and nonreligious and with those less committed to nonviolence. LeRoy Wright argued and fought with everyone to the point that organizers had him bailed him out early.

At midnight on June 15, the riders were thrown into window-less trailer trucks. Two hours later, they emerged to discover that they had been moved one hundred miles northwest to Parchman Prison Farm, perhaps the worst of Mississippi's notorious state penitentiaries.

Parchman was essentially a slave plantation. Hundreds of black convicts guided mule-drawn plows across the 21,000 acres, farming a daily quota of cotton and other crops. Guards kicked, bullwhipped, and cursed at the prisoners.

Superintendent Fred Jones greeted the riders and warned that here there were "bad niggers," some of whom were on death row, who would "beat you up and cut you as soon as look at you." Shotgun-toting guards pushed the riders past barbed wire fences and challenged them to sing songs. When two resisted, the guards laughed and said there weren't any newspapermen out here.

Inside the cement block buildings, deputies stripped the riders naked. Two and a half hours later, a sheriff led them, two by two, into the shower room and ordered them to shave their facial hair. After their shower, they were divided by race and taken to maximum security wings, supposedly to protect them from criminals who wished them ill.

Again they waited naked. An hour and a half later, guards brought them olive green shorts and a t-shirt emblazoned with the words Mississippi State Penitentiary. They deliberately handed out shorts that were either too baggy or too tight.

James Farmer insisted on meeting with the director of prisons. A nearly nude Farmer demanded that they be allowed to work. The director responded that Governor Ross Barnett didn't want them to work.

Barnett was worried about negative press attention, and the riders would be at the mercy of hardened criminals. After voicing this apparent concern, the director admitted that he wanted the riders to stay inside and rot.

Two weeks into the their stay, Governor Barnett gave a tour of the prison and pointed to the riders as an example of what outside instigators faced. The *Jackson Daily News* posted a facetious bulletin stating that tourists promoting race-mixing could stay at Parchman.

The riders' rooms consisted of a metal-frame bed, an inmate-made mattress, one commode, a small washbowl, and no blankets. The only interaction they had with one another was when they showered. The only reading materials allowed were palm-sized

Salvation Army copies of the New Testament. There was no incoming mail, but riders could send a letter once a week. Lewis wrote to let the American Baptist Theological Seminary know why he was to miss graduation.

During hunger strikes, guards tempted them with pecan pie and fried chicken. When fasting ended, riders were served nearly inedible food. The director had also admitted to Farmer that while they were legally required to feed the prisoners, the prisons could put enough salt in the riders' food to make their stomachs turn. Farmer said he lost thirty pounds.

The riders' singing prompted one guard to ask how he could stop their singing if he couldn't "go upside their heads." Instead of beating them, the guards took the riders' mattresses. Hank Thomas declared, "Take my mattress! I'll keep my soul," prompting others to throw their mattresses against the bars. Howard University's Fred Leonard held fast to his mattress as the guards pulled it into the hall. The riders cheered him on as he sang, "I'm Gonna Tell God How You Treat Me."

The guards' tortures continued. They blew cigarette smoke into smokers' cells. Overseers kept the lights on all night and closed the windows when it was hot. They drenched riders with hoses, flooded the cells, and opened the windows. At night, they turned on the fan as riders slept on the wet metal floor.

"Troublemakers" were shocked with cattle prods and placed in sun-baked sweat boxes. Those put in solitary confinement were often bound with wrist-breakers, devices tightened around the wrists. One woman miscarried as a prison guard just watched.

On July 7, the first round of riders were handed their clothes and released to lawyers and friends. They hugged one another, but none cried.

While the SNCC riders were stuck in prison, reinforcements flooded into Jackson. Hundreds of clergymen, communists, rabbis, Quakers, conscientious objectors, pacifists, unionists, and professors made Freedom Rides that summer. Diane Nash had her work cut out for her.

CORE posted a $500 appeal bond for every freedom rider, paying $300,000 in total. The prosecutor almost succeeded in bankrupting them. Farmer told Thurgood Marshall who mentioned that he had set up a NAACP Legal Defense and Education Fund. The fund could help CORE out with between $200,000 and $250,000. Farmer threw his arms around him.

When the riders left Mississippi, the prosecutor ordered that each case be tried in state appeals courts. If the riders didn't return, they had to forfeit their money. Roy Wilkins of the NAACP sent $1,000 to help CORE pay for chartered buses to take riders back to Mississippi. This time, CORE made it clear that the riders had to stay out of jail.

7

Aftermath

The 1961 Freedom Rides had both immediate and longterm consequences across many aspects of American life. One of the most important results may have been symbolic. Dr. Martin Luther King Jr. called the rides "a psychological turning point in our whole struggle." John Lewis called the rides a "monumental event in the movement." The courageous Freedom Riders made such an impression that over the next few years young civil rights workers in the South were often generically referred to as "freedom riders."

Some of the actual riders received celebrity status. A mass rally was held in Pittsburgh to raise funds and "Salute to the Freedom Riders." Queen of Gospel Mahalia Jackson sang, and Dr. King spoke. SCLC presented $500 Freedom Award scholarships to the riders.

Effects within the Movement

The Freedom Rides signaled the coming of a youth movement within the civil rights movement. The sit-ins that began in the 1960s had already inspired the creation of SNCC, the Student Non-Violent Coordinating Committee. The second wave of riders from Nashville were already a part of SNCC and were sit-in veterans.

Young leaders such as John Lewis were ready for future struggles, including voter registration in the South. To a large extent, the Southern-born SCLC and the student-driven SNCC now overshadowed James Farmer's CORE and the NAACP as leading civil rights organizations in the mind of the public. The first part of the civil rights movement was over.

With change came increasing discontent and competition among organizations. The rides were noteworthy for bringing disparate groups together and expressing the democratic spirit at the heart of the movement, but SNCC resented that SCLC and its spokesperson King received credit for the Freedom Rides. Riders felt slightly betrayed when King moved on to other projects.

Nonetheless, the original riders inspired thousands of young people to believe that ordinary citizens could solve political problems. This was a national problem, not just a Southern issue. Students saw what they could accomplish and discovered that they could do it more quickly than the federal government. This outlook influenced protest campaigns throughout the 1960s. The riders' emphasis on nonviolence echoed throughout the world.

Legal Results

Attorney General Robert Kennedy promptly asked the ICC for a directive that would end bus segregation and "declare unequivocally by regulation that a Negro passenger is free to travel the length and breadth of this country in the same manner as any other passenger."

The ICC ruled on September 22 that bus depots had to post signs stating that seating "is without regard to race, color, creed or national origin." By November, bus companies that used segregated terminals would be fined.

Salynn McCollum, who had been taken home from Birmingham by her father, was amongst those who tested ICC's ruling in December. Within three months of ICC's decision, CORE successfully visited eighty-five Southern stations.

In *Lewis v. Greyhound*, U.S. District Judge Frank M. Johnson Jr. declared that Montgomery's segregated facilities were unconstitutional. Attorney Fred Gray had thus won the overturning of the state court injunction against the riders in Alabama. The U.S. Supreme Court subsequently sided with the Freedom Riders against Mississippi, which was forced to refund their bond money. In 1965, the Court completely cleared all Freedom Riders' records.

The Freedom Riders had won a complete, public victory against segregated travel. Interracial groups could travel across the country and use the same waiting rooms and restaurants. Bus and train stations removed "whites-only" signs that had stood for decades.

The rides awoke the nation and the federal government to the lengths segregationists went to maintain the status quo. They forced the Kennedy administration to pay attention to civil rights issues. Though it was a rough ride, the government had sided with the protesters, and the Justice Department upheld federal regulations.

Increased Militancy

The next decade would witness increasing militancy from both extreme segregationists and from some civil rights leaders.

The mid-1960s saw an explosion of bombings, beatings, assassinations, crossburnings, and other acts of intimidation by members of the Ku Klux Klan and other violence-prone white supremacist groups.

Meanwhile, black nationalists like Stokely Carmichael contributed to the radicalization of the civil rights movement. The nineteen-year-old Carmichael had flown from New York to join the freedom riders in Mississippi's prisons. Carmichael took over SNCC in 1966. He changed his name to Kwame Ture and moved SNCC away from nonviolence and towards black power.

Turning Point in Montgomery

As for Montgomery, the Freedom Rides shocked the city into belated progress. Businessman Winton Blount played a key role in this change of climate. He pressed civic groups to publicly condemn the violence against the Freedom Riders. Montgomery's Rotary Club unanimously adopted a resolution criticizing police inaction, as did the more reluctant Kiwanis Club. Blount convinced the Alabama State Chamber of Commerce's board of directors to strongly assert the necessity of law enforcement. They stated that the violent reactions in Alabama damaged the state's reputation and business opportunities. The white Montgomery Ministerial Association and the Junior Chamber of Commerce also formally disapproved of the city's law enforcement officials. This response contrasted with, as *Montgomery Advertiser* editor Grover Hall wrote, the white community's previously "silent and passive" reaction "in the teeth of local violence."

In 1962, the federal court banned segregation in Montgomery's public museums, libraries, and airports. Alabama's capital didn't shut down all its public facilities in petty response. This time, the city chose peaceful integration.

In 1963, Blount, a University of Alabama trustee, contacted Robert Kennedy when Governor George Wallace vowed to prohibit two black students from attending. They reached a compromise, allowing Wallace to have his say but requiring that he step aside and let the students enroll.

Blount later became President Richard Nixon's postmaster general and a well-regarded philanthropist. He saved and expanded the Alabama Shakespeare Festival, contributed heavily to the Montgomery Museum of Fine Art, and built a large park surrounding the theater and museum. Blount also donated to numerous education programs.

In the upcoming years, Montgomery's relative acceptance of desegregation contrasted with Birmingham's enduring belligerence, partly due to the Freedom Riders' dramatic reception and Winton Blount's calming influence.

Next Decade

The rides sent a message to the South. The country's next decade would involve a tumultuous wrestling match between progress and resistance. War protests, equality marches, Civil Rights Acts, voting legislation, violence, and the assassinations of President John F. Kennedy, his brother Attorney General Robert Kennedy, and Dr. Martin Luther King Jr. all deeply affected the United States.

8

FREEDOM RIDE MUSEUMS AND MEMORIALS

Anniston, Alabama

A historical marker commemorates the site on Route 202, near Hunter Street, where a Greyhound bus carrying freedom riders was forced to the side of the road and attacked by a KKK-led mob on May 14, 1961.

Birmingham, Alabama

The Birmingham Civil Rights Institute has a gallery telling the story of the Freedom Rides, including a short film, photos, and a replica of the burned Greyhound bus. The BCRI is at 520 Sixteenth Street North, Birmingham, AL 35203. Admission charged. http://www.bcri.org.

The freedom riders were attacked at the Trailways bus station that was located at Nineteenth Street and Fourth Avenue North. A historical marker indicates the site now.

Freedom rider reinforcements left for Montgomery from the Greyhound bus station at 2316 Seventh Avenue North, Birmingham, AL 35203.

Montgomery, Alabama

The Greyhound bus station where riders were beaten has been converted into a museum dedicated to the Freedom Rides. Only partially completed as of May 2011, the museum already features an award-winning exterior exhibit, interior exhibits, a story quilt, and a Share Your Story kiosk for recording reactions from visitors, witnesses, and riders. The site is at 210 South Court Street, Montgomery, AL 36104. Free. http://www.preserveala.org

The Trailways bus station, from which riders departed for Jackson, has been converted to offices for the Alabama Gas Corporation. The address is 221 Lee St., Montgomery, AL 36104.

Jim Zwerg and William Barbee were treated at the City of St. Jude Hospital. Harold Purcell, an Irish Catholic priest from New Jersey, founded the complex in predominantly black west Montgomery where he thought the need for education, medical care, and social services was greatest. The grounds of the complex would be in the news again in 1965 when the Selma-to-Montgomery marchers camped there on the last night of the march. The hospital is now a senior citizens housing facility, but the complex still exists at 2048 West Fairview Avenue, Montgomery, AL 36108. http://www.cityofstjude.com.

The First Baptist Church, the site of the mass meeting following the freedom riders' arrival, is one of the oldest black churches in Montgomery. In 1961. The Reverend Ralph Abernathy, close friend of Dr. Martin Luther King Jr., was its minister in 1961, as he was during the Montgomery bus boycott when the church was bombed by KKK members. The church remains an active house of worship today. It is located at 347 North Ripley Street, Montgomery, AL 36104.

Dr. Richard Harris lived two houses down from the parsonage of the Dexter Avenue Baptist Church and was thus a neighbor of Dr. Martin Luther King Jr. during King's five years in Montgomery. Harris's home was a place of refuge for activists. It is now a private residence at 333 South Jackson Street, Montgomery, AL 36104.

Only days after he was attacked, John Lewis testified before Judge Frank M. Johnson at the federal courthouse adjacent to the

Greyhound bus station. Johnson's courtroom has been preserved and can be visited by prior arrangement. 1 Church Street, Montgomery, AL 36104.

The Alabama Capitol, where Governor John Patterson conferred by phone and in person with federal officials over the Freedom Riders, stands at Bainbridge Street and Dexter Avenue in downtown Montgomery.

Jackson, Mississippi

The former Greyhound station where the Freedom Riders were arrested on arrival is located at 219 North Lamar St., Jackson, MS 39201.

A planetarium now sits where Jackson's Trailways station was located at 201 East Pascagoula Street, Jackson, MS 39201.

The freedom riders were thrown into the Hinds County Detention Center at 407 East Pascagoula Street, Jackson, MS 39201.

Parchman Prison is located near Parchman, Mississippi, in rural Sunflower County.

Memphis, Tennessee

The National Civil Rights Museum houses a permanent Freedom Riders exhibit at 450 Mulberry St., Memphis, TN 38103. Admission charged. http://www.civilrightsmuseum.org

9

SOURCES AND
FURTHER READING

Arsenault, Ray. *Freedom Riders: 1961 and the Struggle for Racial Justice.* New York: Oxford UP, 2006.

Branch, Taylor. *Parting the Waters: America in the King Years 1954-63.* New York: Simon & Schuster, 1988.

Bausum, Ann. *Freedom Riders: John Lewis and Jim Zwerg on the Front Lines of the Civil Rights Movement.* Washington, D.C.: National Geographic Society, 2006.

Encyclopedia of Alabama: http://www.encyclopediaofalabama.org/face/Article.jsp?id=h-1637.

Lewis, John, and Michael D'Orso. *Walking with the Wind: A Memoir of the Movement.* New York: Harcourt Brace & Co., 1999.

Noble, Phil. *Beyond the Burning Bus: The Civil Rights Revolution in a Southern Town.* Montgomery: NewSouth Books, 2003.

Raines, Howell. *My Soul Is Rested: The Story of the Civil Rights Movement in the Deep South.* New York: Penguin Books, 1983.

Thornton, J. Mills, III. *Dividing Lines: Municipal Politics and the Struggle for Civil Rights in Montgomery, Birmingham, and Selma.* Tuscaloosa, Alabama: University of Alabama Press, 2002.

Thornton, J. Mills, and Joseph Caver. *Touched by History: A Self-Guided Tour to Civil Rights Sites in Central Alabama, Special Montgomery Edition with an Alabama State University Supplement.* Montgomery: NewSouth Books, 2005.

Williams, Juan. *Eyes on the Prize: America's Civil Rights Years, 1954-1965.* New York: Penguin Books, 2002.

Williams, Horace Randall, and Ben Beard. *This Day in Civil Rights History.* Montgomery: NewSouth Books, 2009

Zellner, Bob. *The Wrong Side of Murder Creek: A White Southerner in the Freedom Movement.* Montgomery: NewSouth Books, 2008.

INDEX

Student Nonviolent Coordinating
Committee. *See* SNCC
Student Voice, The 33
Sullivan, L. B. 48, 52–53, 61
Sumter, South Carolina 6

T

Tennessee 5, 24, 30, 44, 67, 84
Tennessee State University 42, 67
Thomas, Hank 6, 33, 39, 55, 67, 71,
   73, 75
Thomas, Max 73
Thompson, Jean 73
Thompson, Myron 10
Thurmond, Strom 26
Todd, Curtiss 24
Tourgee, Albion 17
Trailways stations 22, 23, 31, 39–40,
   69–70, 82–84
Trailways Transportation System 22,
   23, 32, 35
Trillin, Calvin 49
Troy, Alabama 51
Truman, Harry 17–18, 19
Truth, Sojourner 16
Ture, Kwame. *See* Carmichael,
   Stokely

U

United Press International 45, 59
University of Alabama 27, 80
University of North Carolina 23
University of Texas at El Paso 10
Urbock, Don 50
U.S. Justice Department 40, 41, 47,
   49, 52, 64, 79
U.S. Navy 33
U.S. News & World Report 72
U.S. Supreme Court 17, 21, 22, 24,
   26, 31, 72, 79

V

Vienna, Virginia 57
Virginia 5, 17, 22, 26, 27, 31, 34
Virginia Union College 22
Vivian, C. T. 70, 72, 73

W

Waldron, George 52
Walker, Wyatt Tee 58, 61, 66, 67, 69
Wallace, George 80
Warren, Earl 26
Washington, D.C. 5, 18, 22, 24, 33,
   52, 58, 68
Weaversville, North Carolina 5
West Virginia 5
White Citizens Council 27, 52
Wilbur, Susan 42, 51, 54
Wilkins, Roy 67, 76
Williams, Robert 67
Winnsboro, South Carolina 6
Winston-Salem, North Carolina 5
Wisconsin 43
Woodard, Isaac 19
World War II 17, 18, 33
Worthy, William 22
Wright, LeRoy 73
Wright, Nathan 21, 24
WSFA-TV 56

Z

Zellner, Bob 56, 85
Zwerg, James 42–44, 45, 50, 51,
   53–56, 68, 83

*How the arrival of the Freedom Riders
forever changed the city of Anniston, Alabama ...*

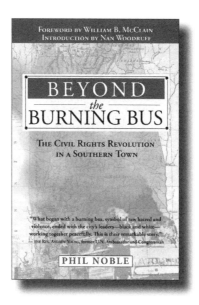

When the Ku Klux Klan firebombed a Freedom Riders bus in Anniston, Alabama, it inspired the black and white leaders of the small industrial city to make a change. Deciding it was better to unite the community than to divide it, the residents of Anniston created a biracial Human Relations Council which set about to quietly dismantle Jim Crow segregation laws and customs.

Author Phil Noble, one of the Council's first leaders, tells his personal story as a resident of Anniston, backed up by well-researched history. *Beyond the Burning Bus* offers a first-hand view of the Freedom Ride and its effects.

ISBN 978-1-58838-120-0
Available in hardcover and ebook formats
Visit www.newsouthbooks.com/beyondtheburningbus

The autobiography of the lawyer who represented the Freedom Riders in Montgomery . . .

Fred Gray, one of two black lawyers in Montgomery, Alabama in 1954, was "determined to destroy everything segregated that I could find." He did not have to wait long. When his friend Rosa Parks was arrested in 1955 for challenging segregation on a city bus, the twenty-four-year-old became her and then Martin Luther King Jr.'s lawyer. He went on to become one of the nation's most successful civil rights lawyers. His clients included the Freedom Riders, the Selma-to-Montgomery marchers, the victims of the Tuskegee Syphilis Study, and many more. *Bus Ride to Justice* is the story of a courageous human being filled with a passion for equal justice.

ISBN 978-1-58838-113-2
Available in paperback
Visit www.newsouthbooks.com/busride

*The federal judge whose ruling validated the
Freedom Riders' purpose . . .*

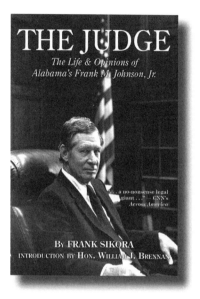

U.S. District Judge Frank Minis Johnson Jr. of Montgomery, Alabama, presided over some of the most significant civil rights cases of the 1950s through the 1970s—and issued rulings that upheld the Constitution and extended equal rights to black citizens, abused prisoners and mental patients, women, and others who sought the freedoms that are the legacy of all Americans. *The Judge* covers many of his notable cases: the Montgomery Bus Boycott, the Freedom Rides, school desegregation, and more. Much of the book consists of extended oral history interviews with Judge Johnson, making this account of his life and career as near an autobiography as exists.

ISBN 978-1-58838-158-3
Available in hardcover
Visit www.newsouthbooks.com/thejudge

Solomon Seay's quest for equality and civil rights, for his clients and himself...

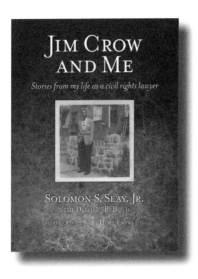

Attorney Solomon S. Seay Jr.'s memoir *Jim Crow and Me: Stories from My Life as a Civil Rights Lawyer* chronicles both heartening and heartbreaking episodes of his first-hand struggle to defeat segregation, including his encounter with the Freedom Riders. Seay relays his personal struggles with fervor and introspection, but he also acknowledges in each of these brief essays the greater societal struggle in which his story is necessarily framed. *Jim Crow and Me* is a rich and readable testament to the tensions and dangers faced by the lawyers who represented in the courtrooms the causes of those who marched and demonstrated in the streets.

ISBN 978-1-58838-175-0
Available in hardcover
Visit www.newsouthbooks.com/seay

*A young white minister thrust by circumstance
into a lifelong commitment to human rights . . .*

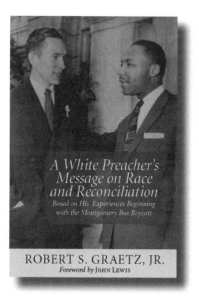

In 1955, when the Montgomery Bus Boycott began, author
Robert Graetz was the young white pastor of a black Lu-
theran Church in Montgomery. His church and his home
were in the black community and he and his wife among the
few local whites who supported the boycott. Their church
and home were bombed; their lives were threatened often.
Graetz never wavered, and those early experiences shaped a
long ministerial career that emphasized equality and justice.
In addition to Graetz's boycott memoirs, *A White Preacher's
Message on Race and Reconciliation* includes chapters on the
present challenges for human and civil rights.

ISBN 978-1-58838-190-3
Available in hardcover and ebook formats
Visit www.newsouthbooks.com/graetz

The larger-than-life story of unlikely civil rights activist Bob Zellner . . .

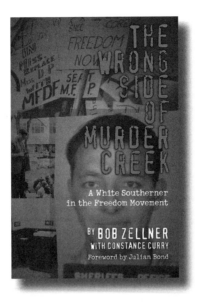

Even forty years after the civil rights movement, the transition from son and grandson of Klansmen to field secretary of SNCC seems quite a journey. In his long-awaited memoir, Bob Zellner tells how one white Alabamian joined ranks with the black students who were sitting-in, marching, fighting, and sometimes dying to challenge the Southern "way of life" he had been raised on but rejected. He was in all the campaigns and was close to all the major figures. *The Wrong Side of Murder Creek*, winner of the 2009 Lillian Smith Book Award, is Bob Zellner's more-amazing-than-fiction story, and it was worth waiting for.

ISBN 978-1-58838-222-1
Available in hardcover and ebook formats
Visit www.newsouthbooks.com/murdercreek